AF251128

EDITED BY MIRJAM VARADINIS

STEFAN BANZ

THE MUHAMMAD ALI'S

VERLAG FÜR MODERNE KUNST NÜRNBERG

"I'm bad, been chopping trees. ... I have wrestled with the alligator. I done tussle with the whale. I done handcuff lightning, thrown thunder in jail. That's bad. Only last week I murdered a rock, injured a stone, hospitalized a brick. I'm so mean, I make medicine sick."

Muhammad Ali

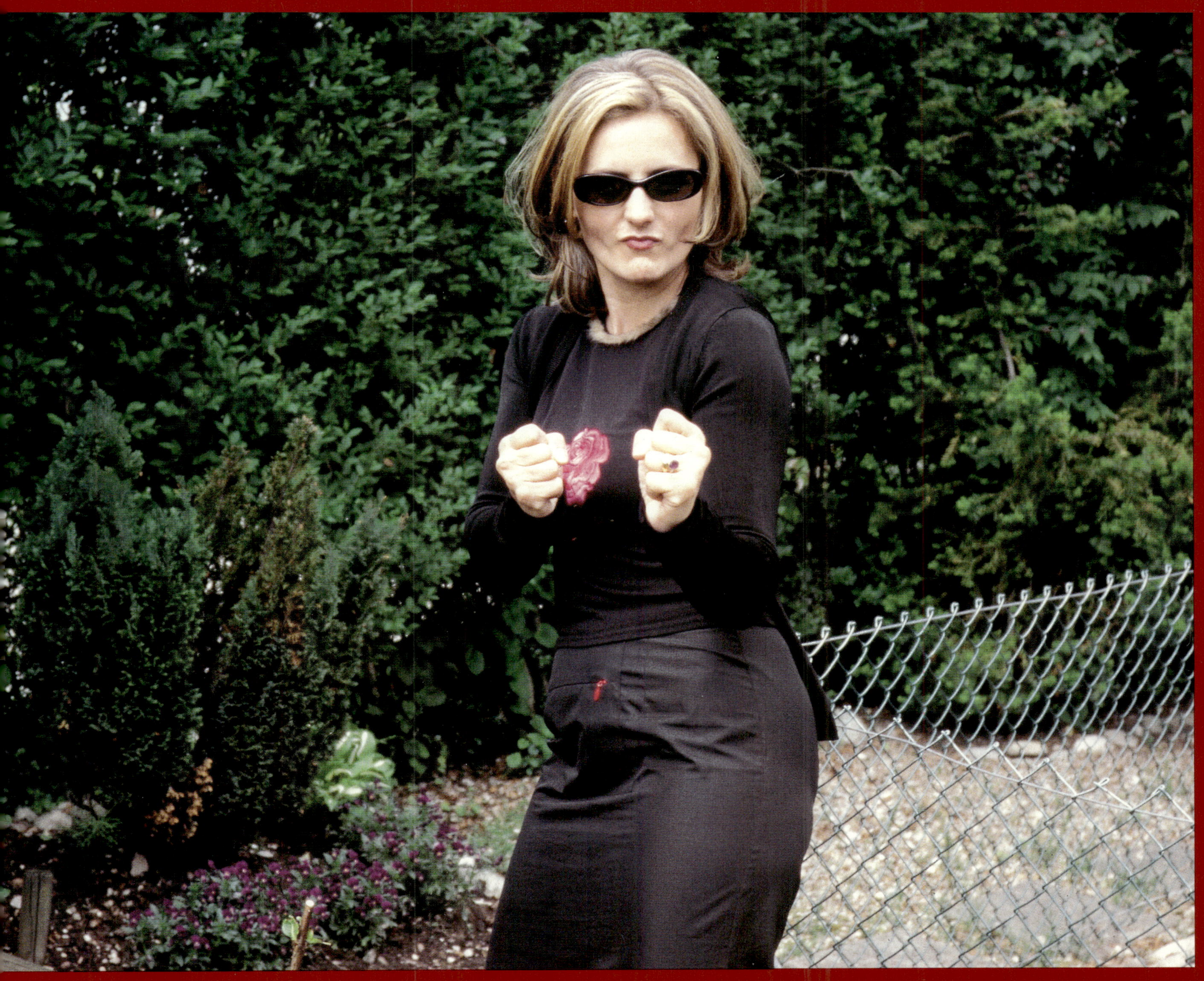

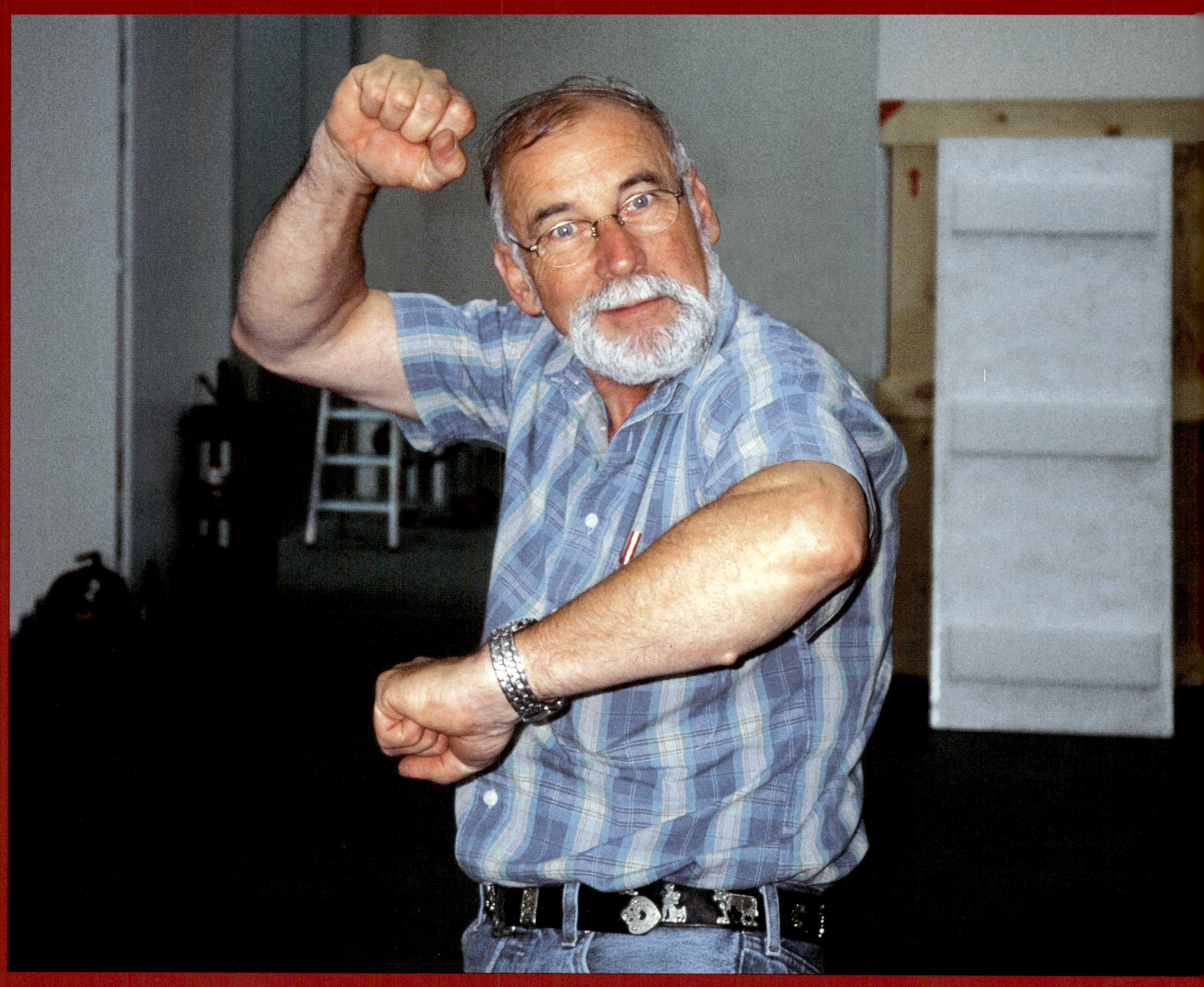

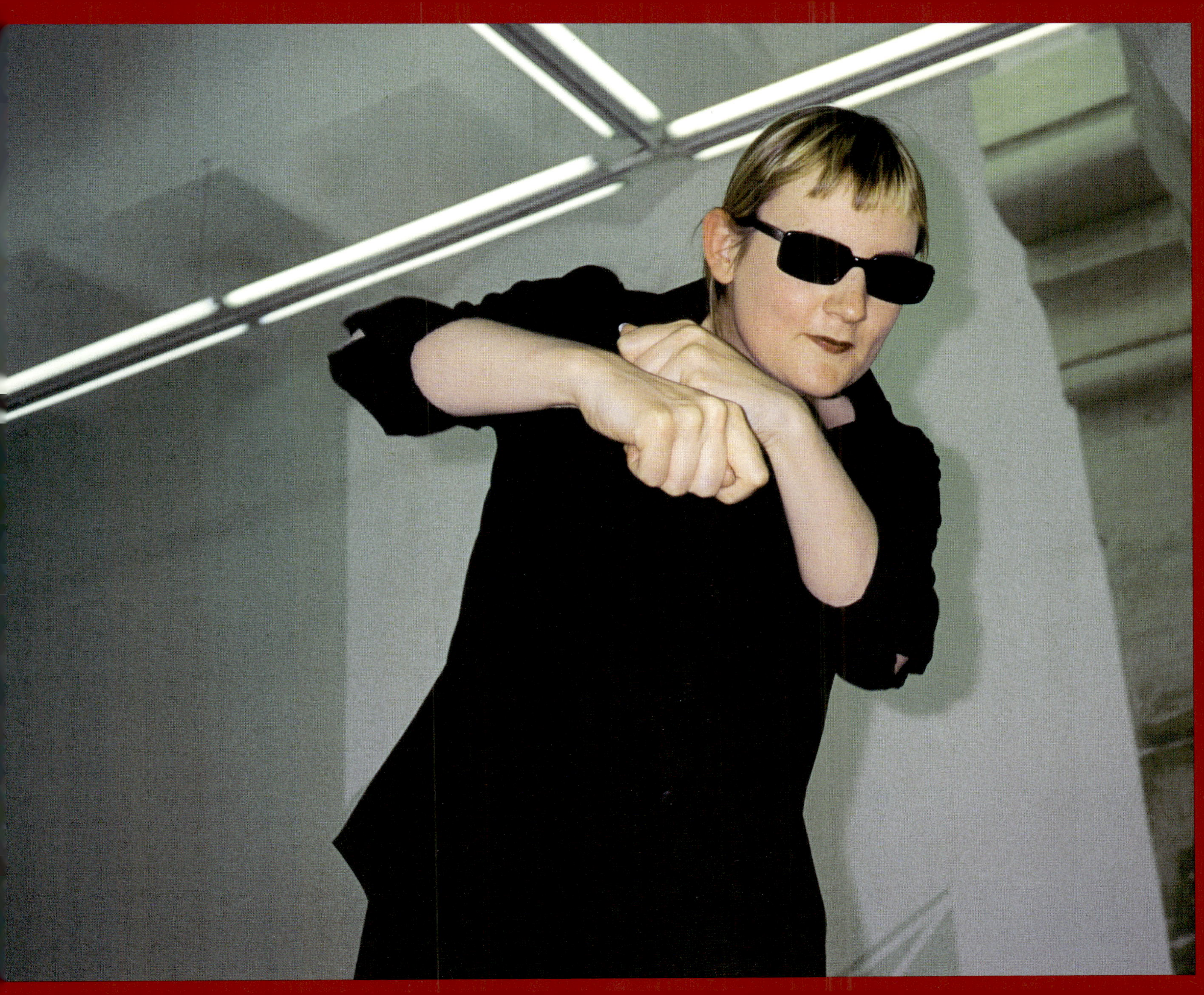

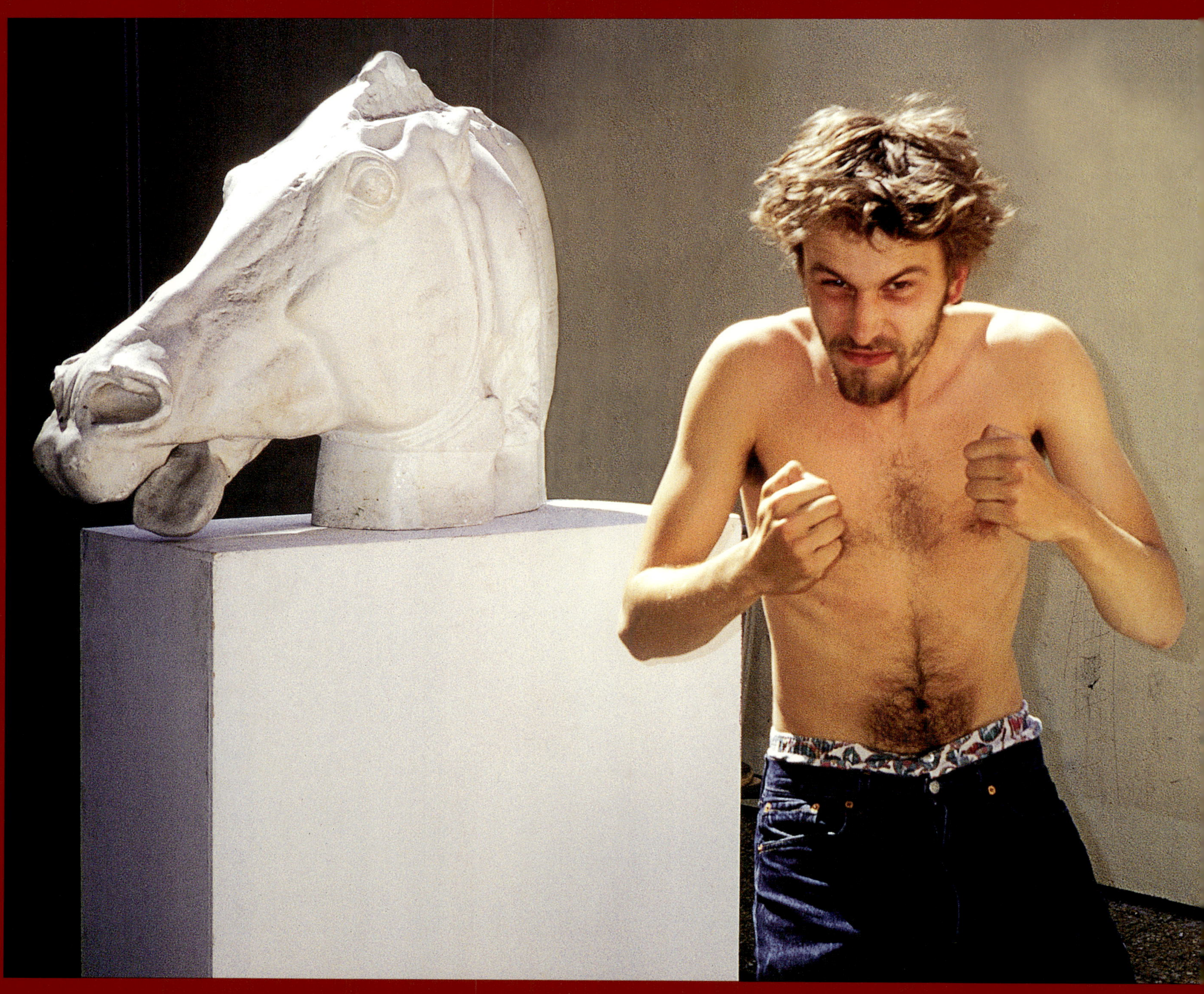

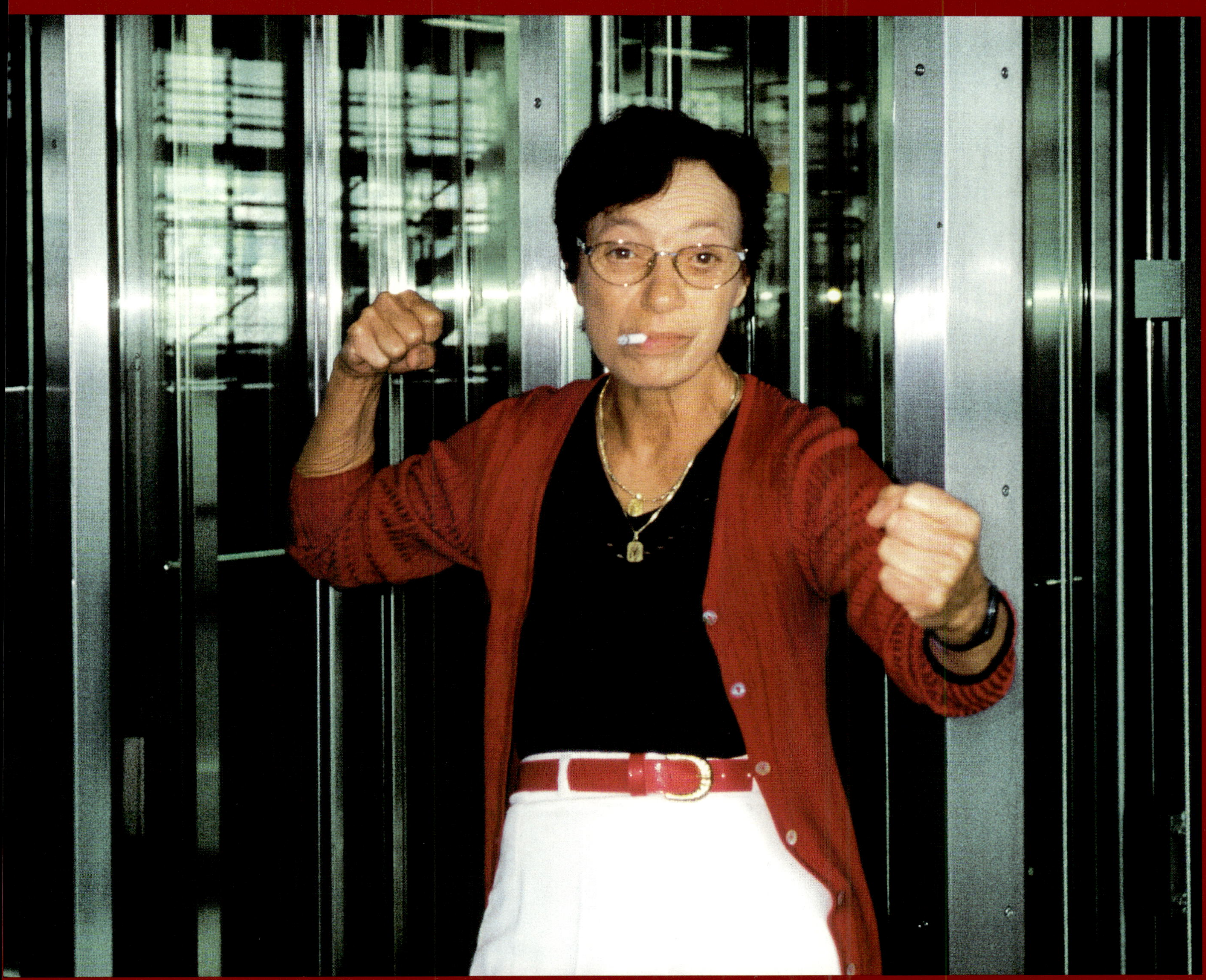

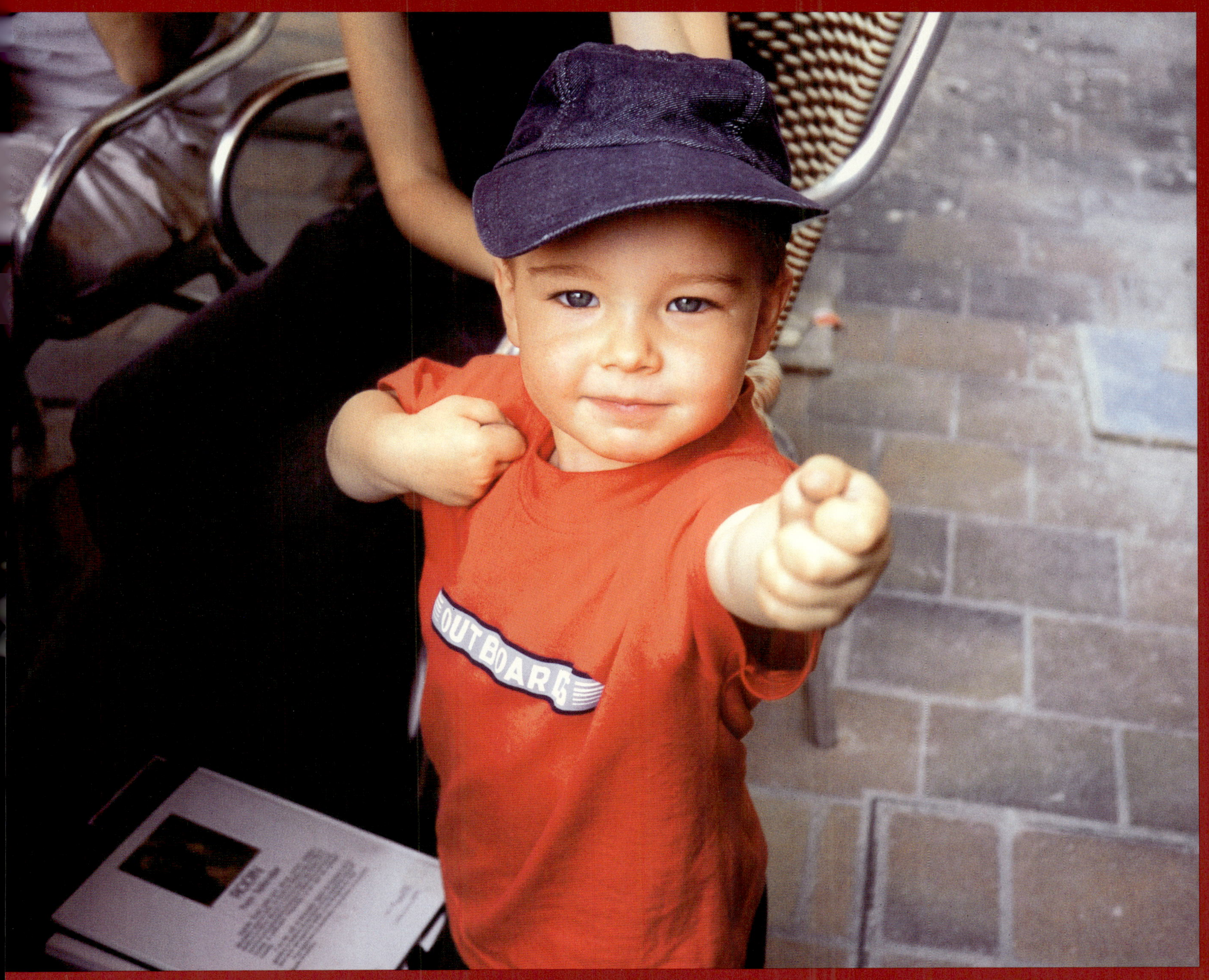

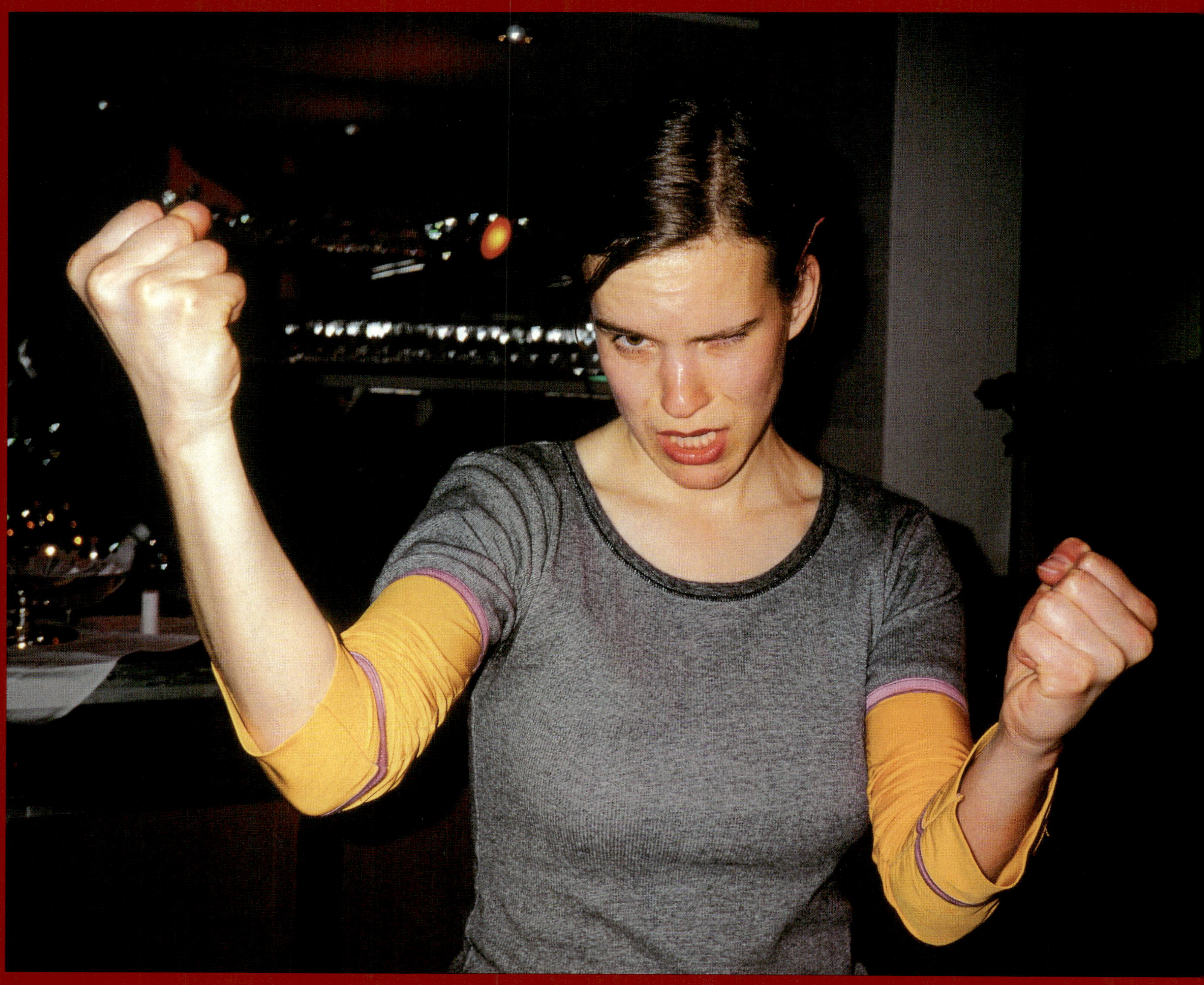

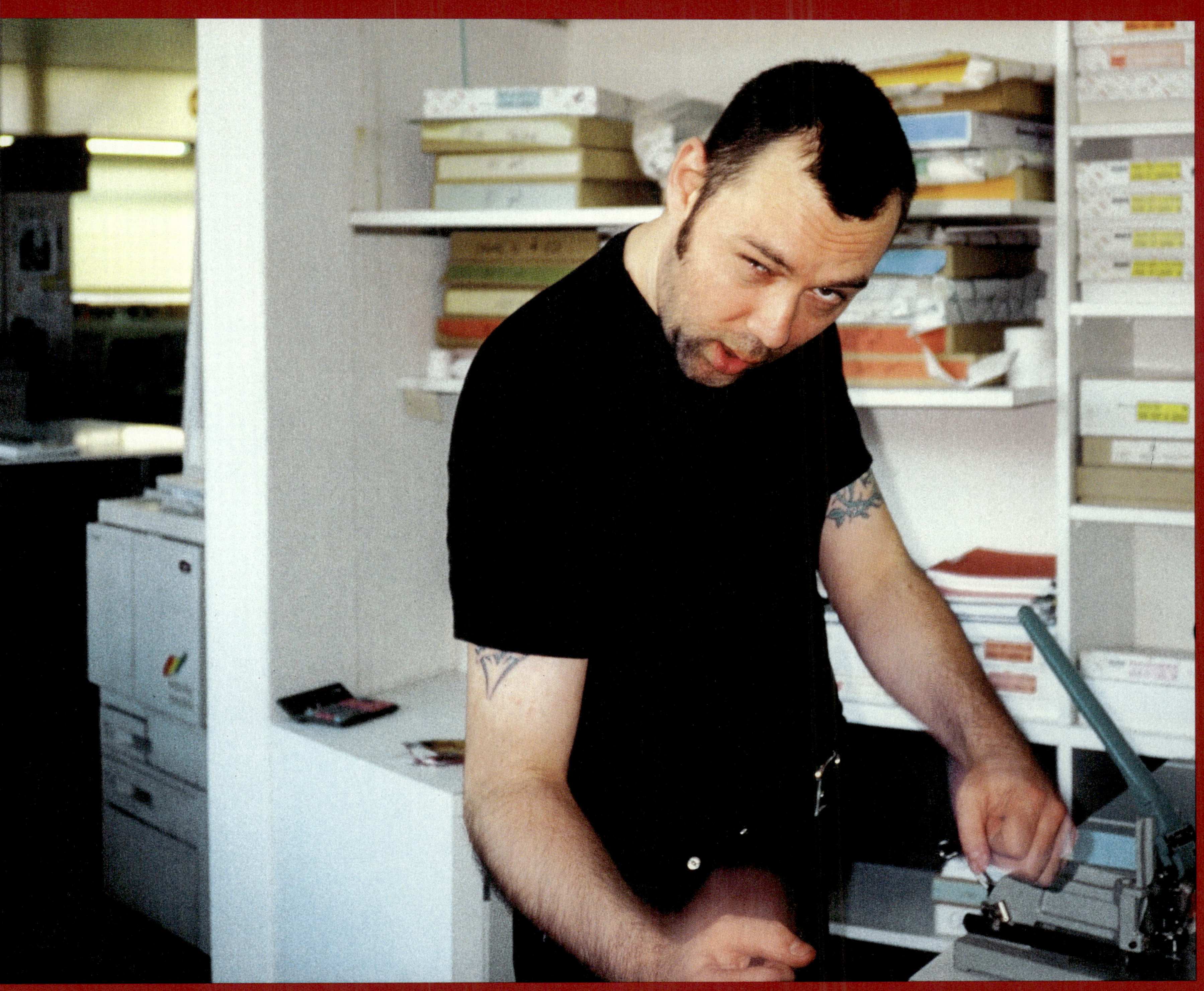

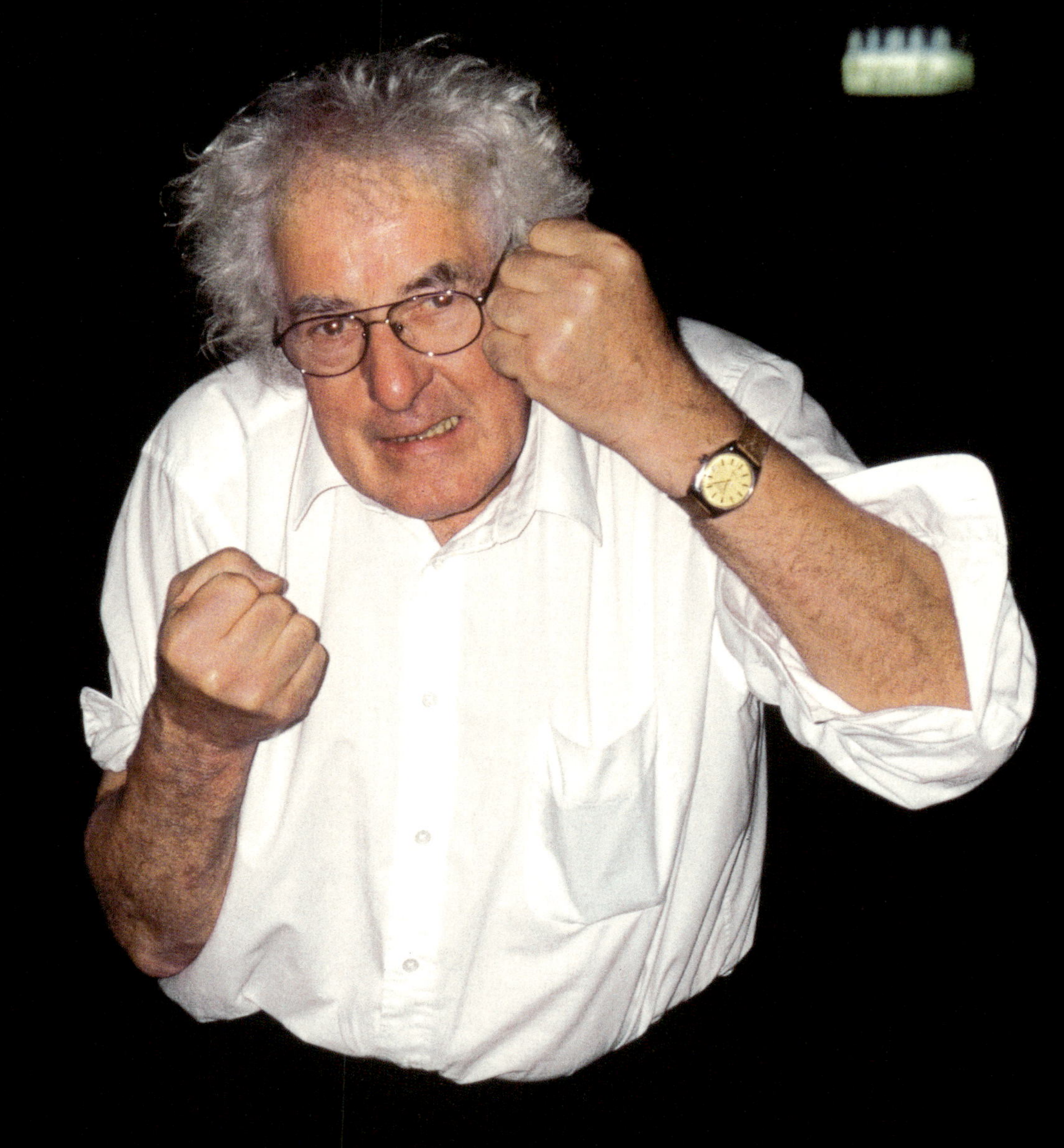

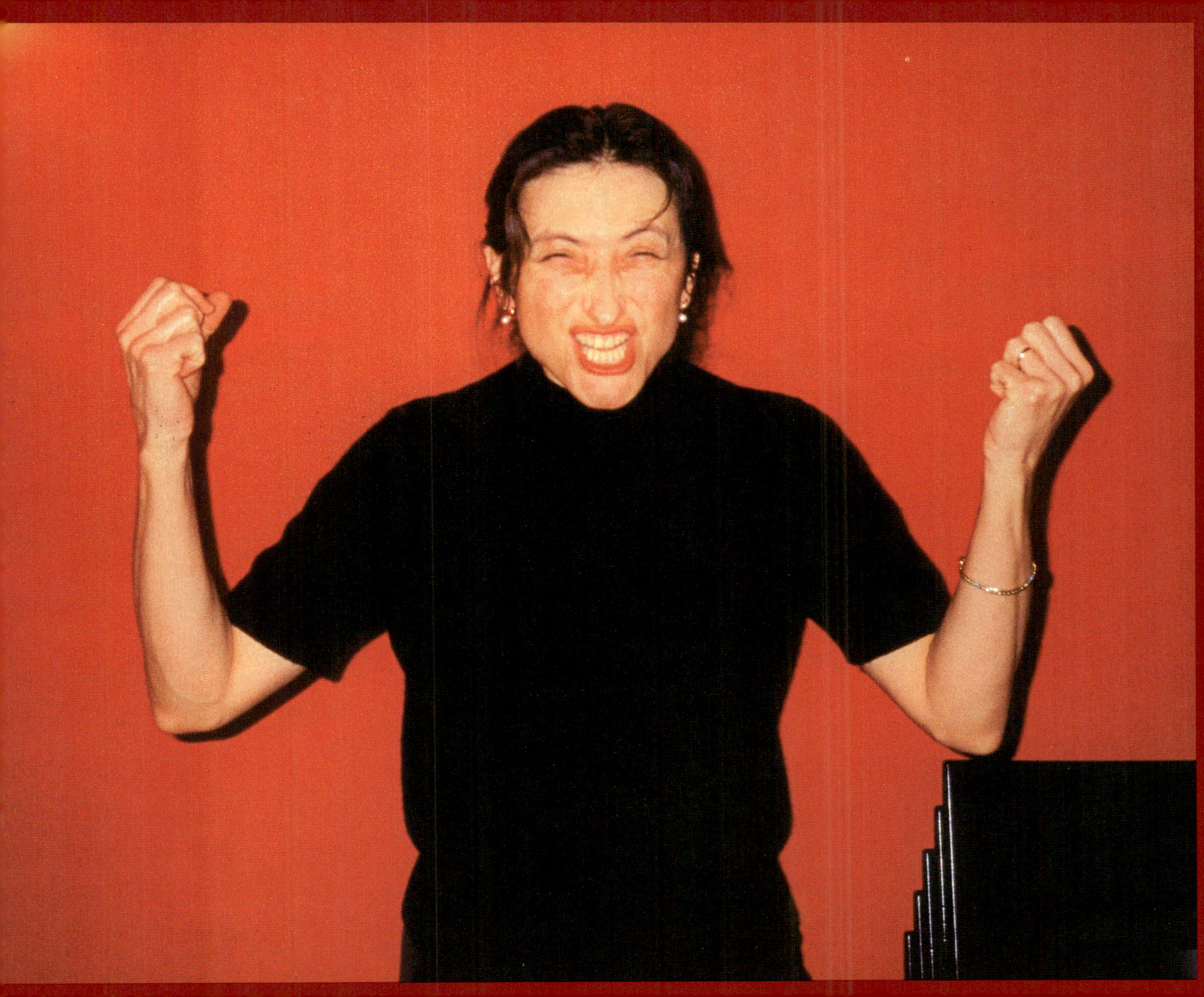

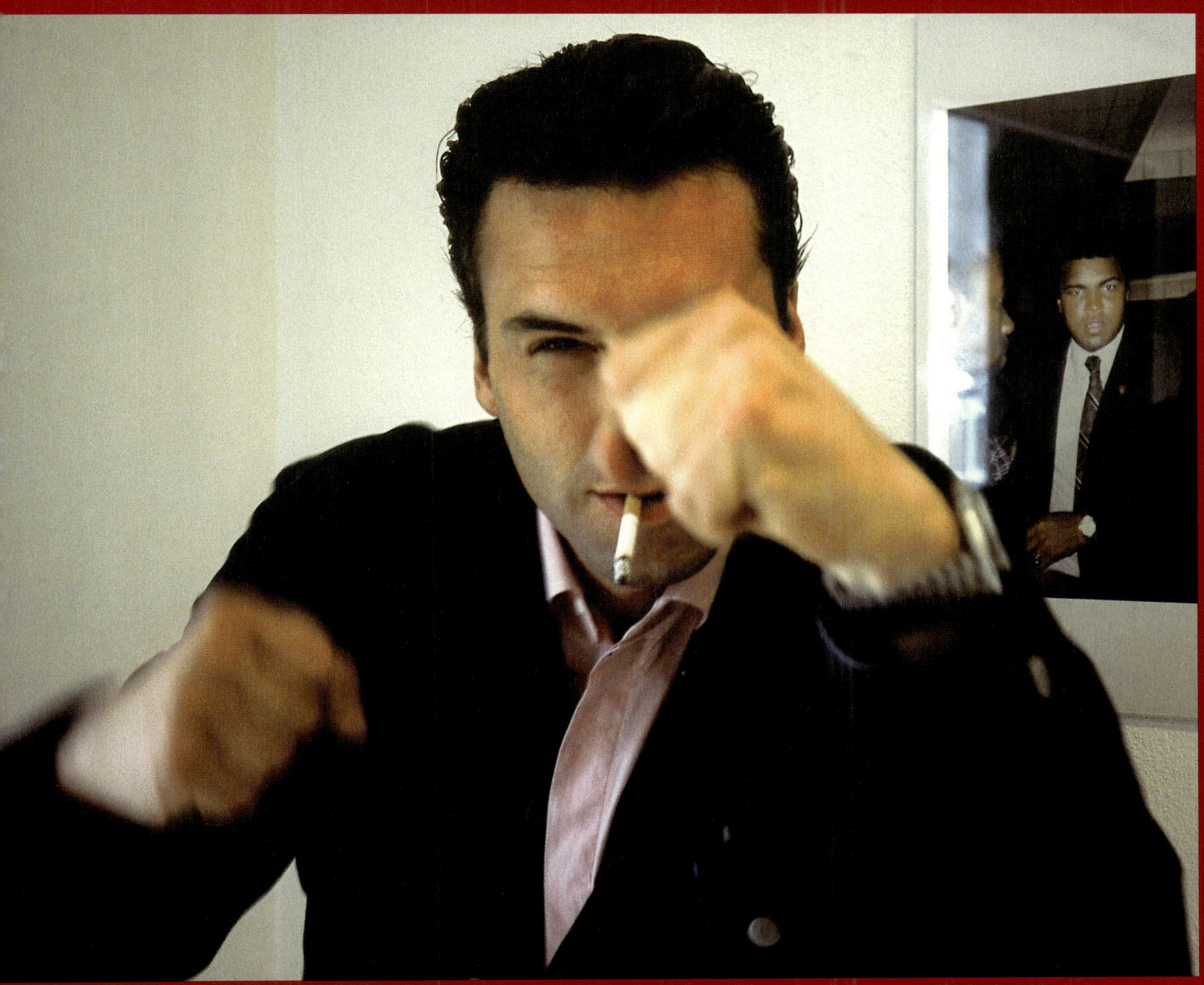

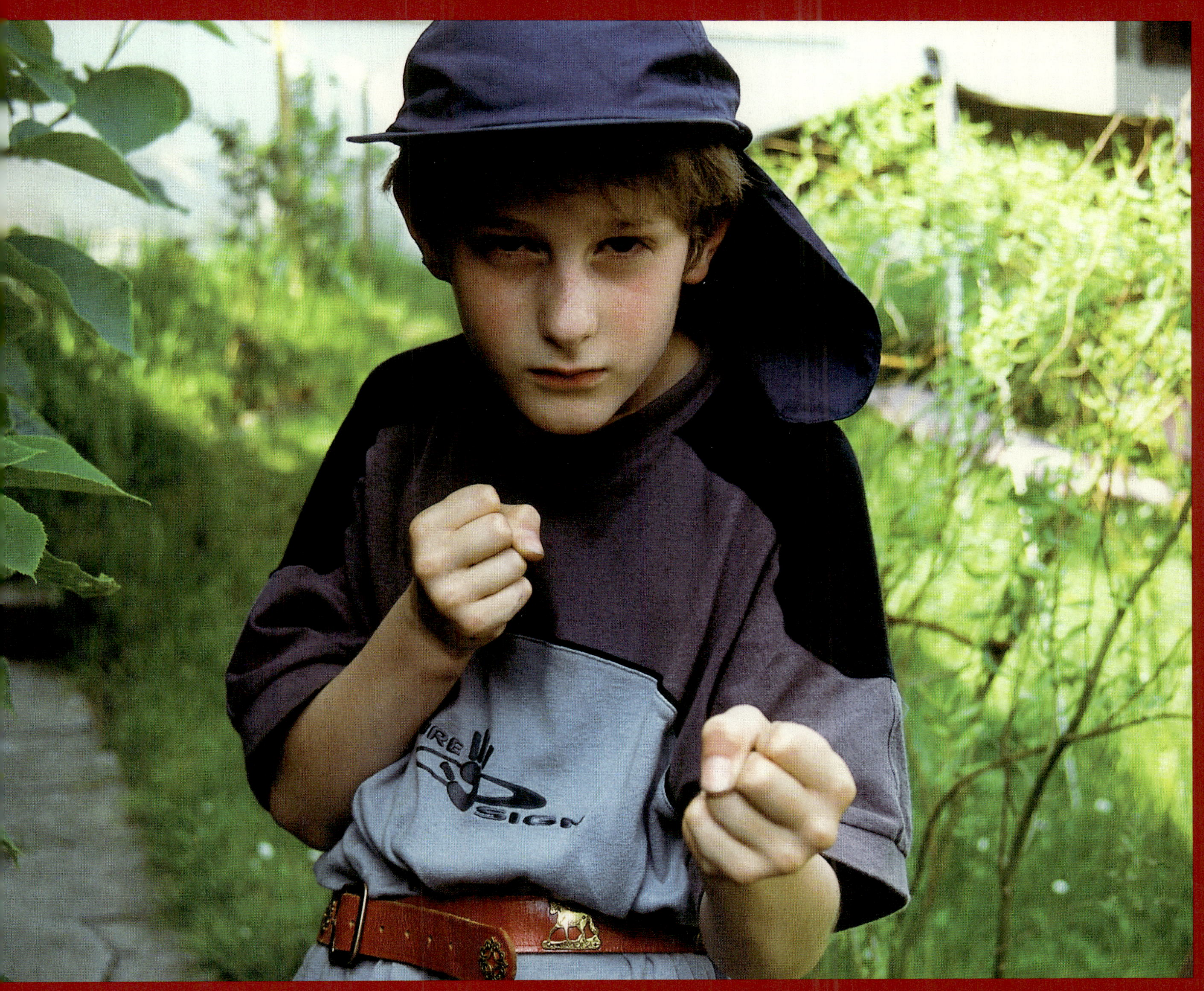

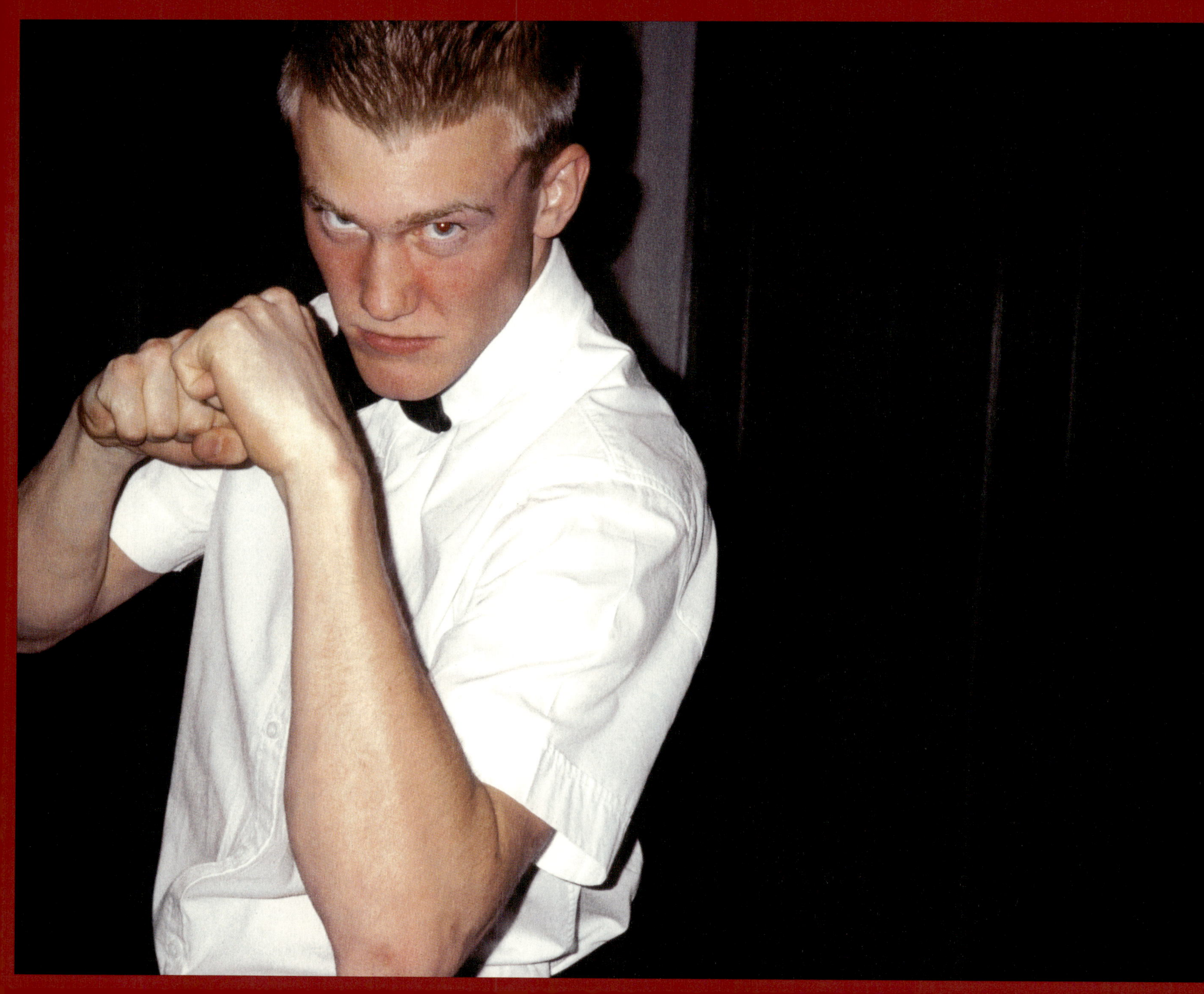

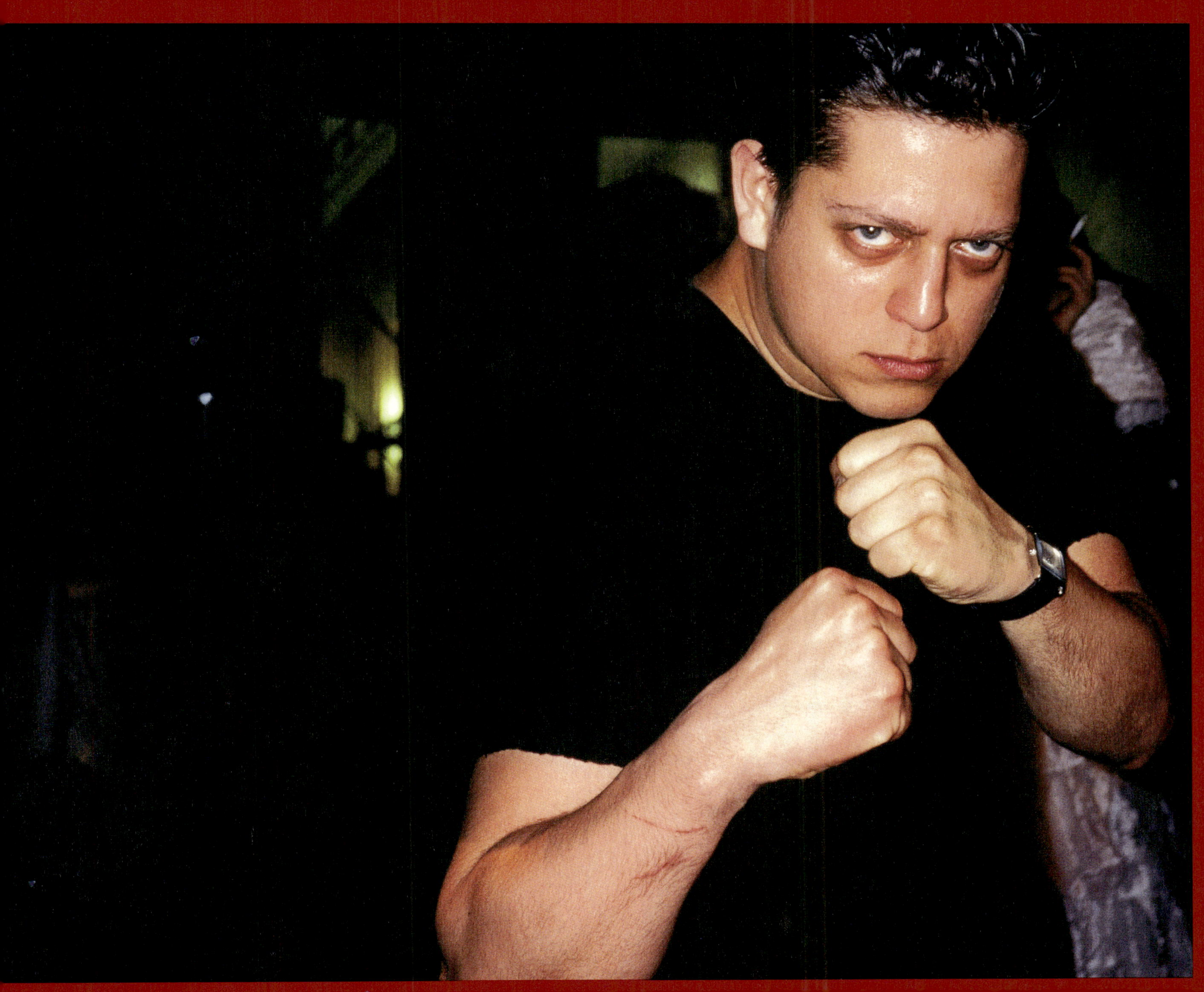

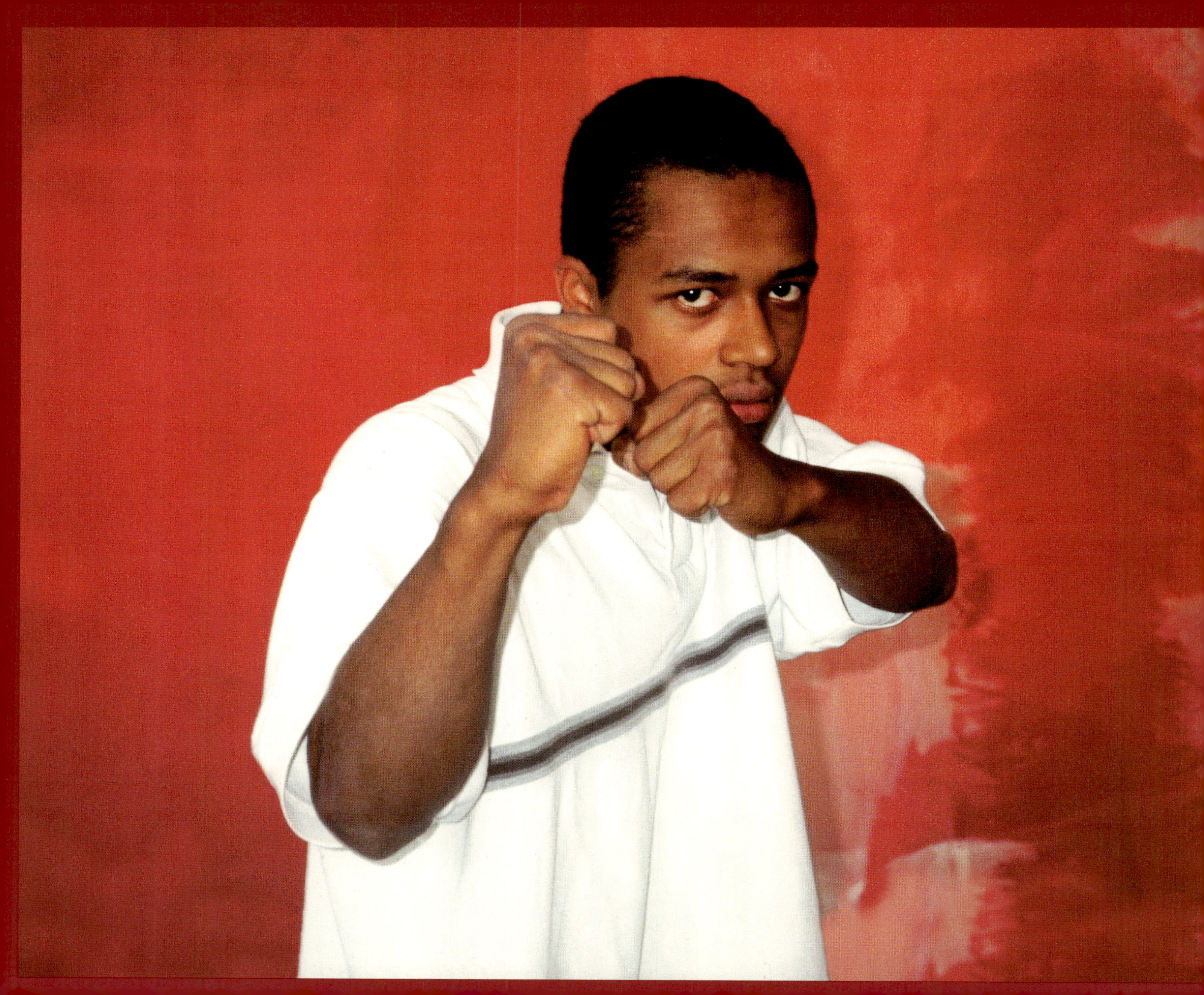

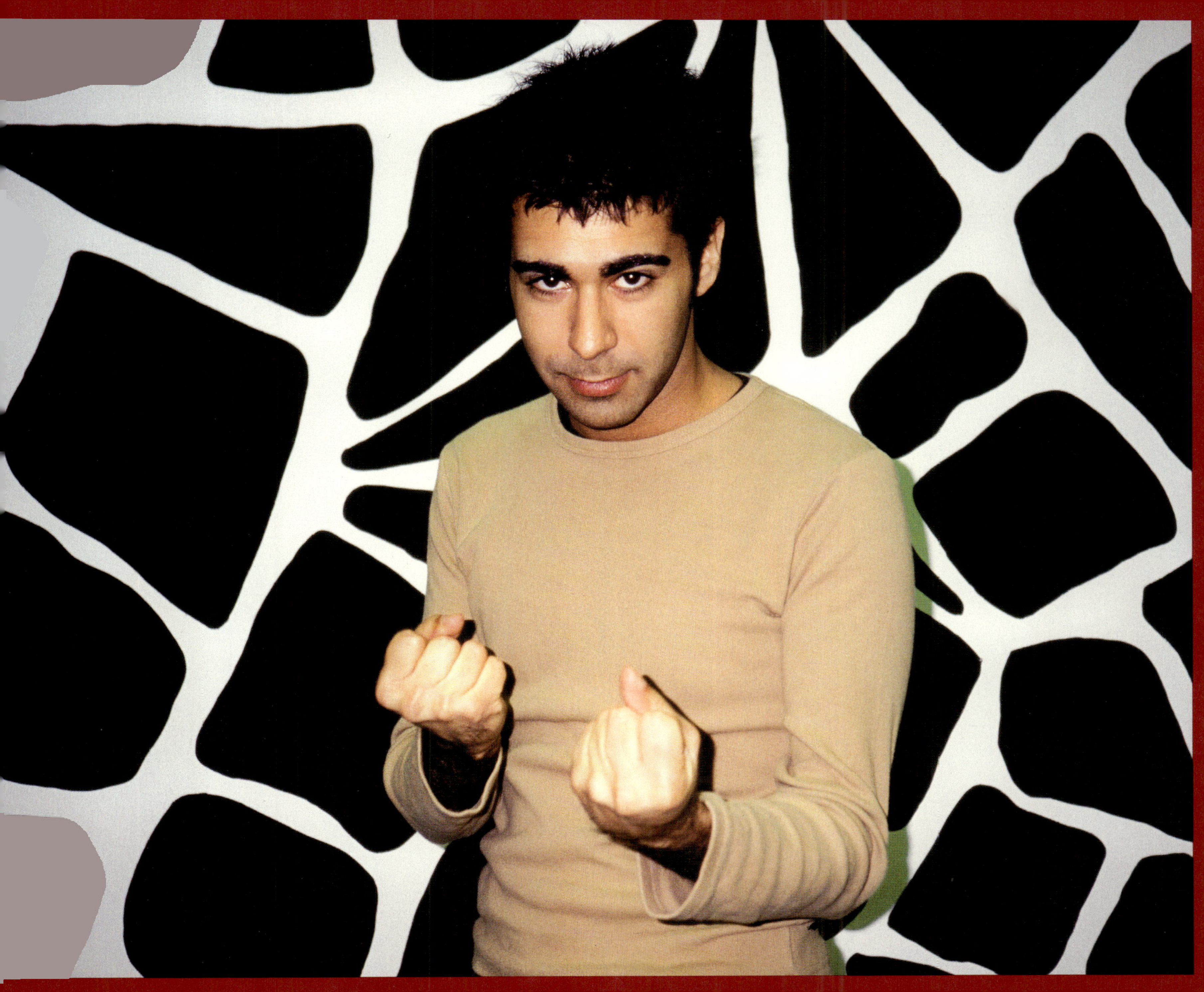

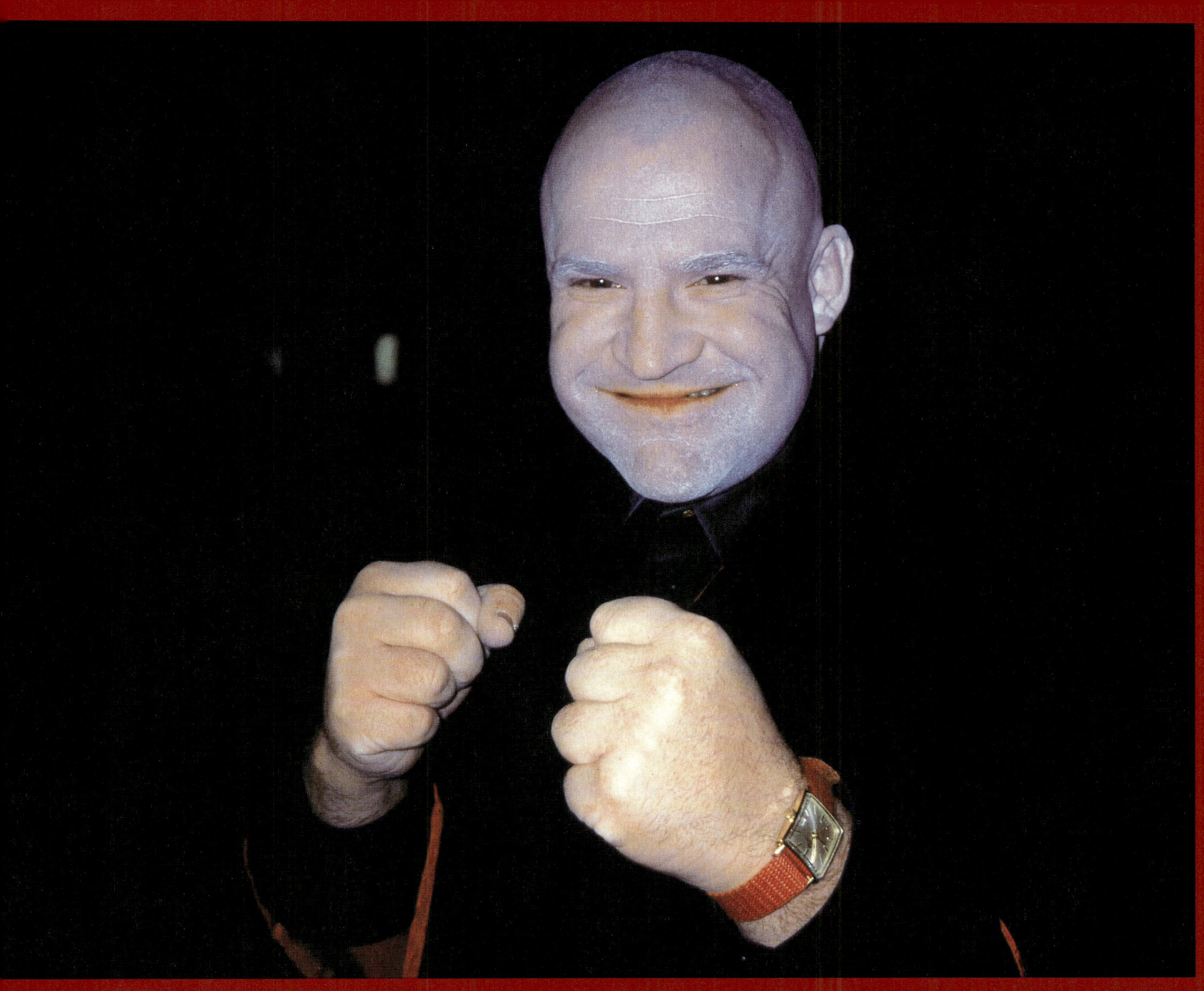

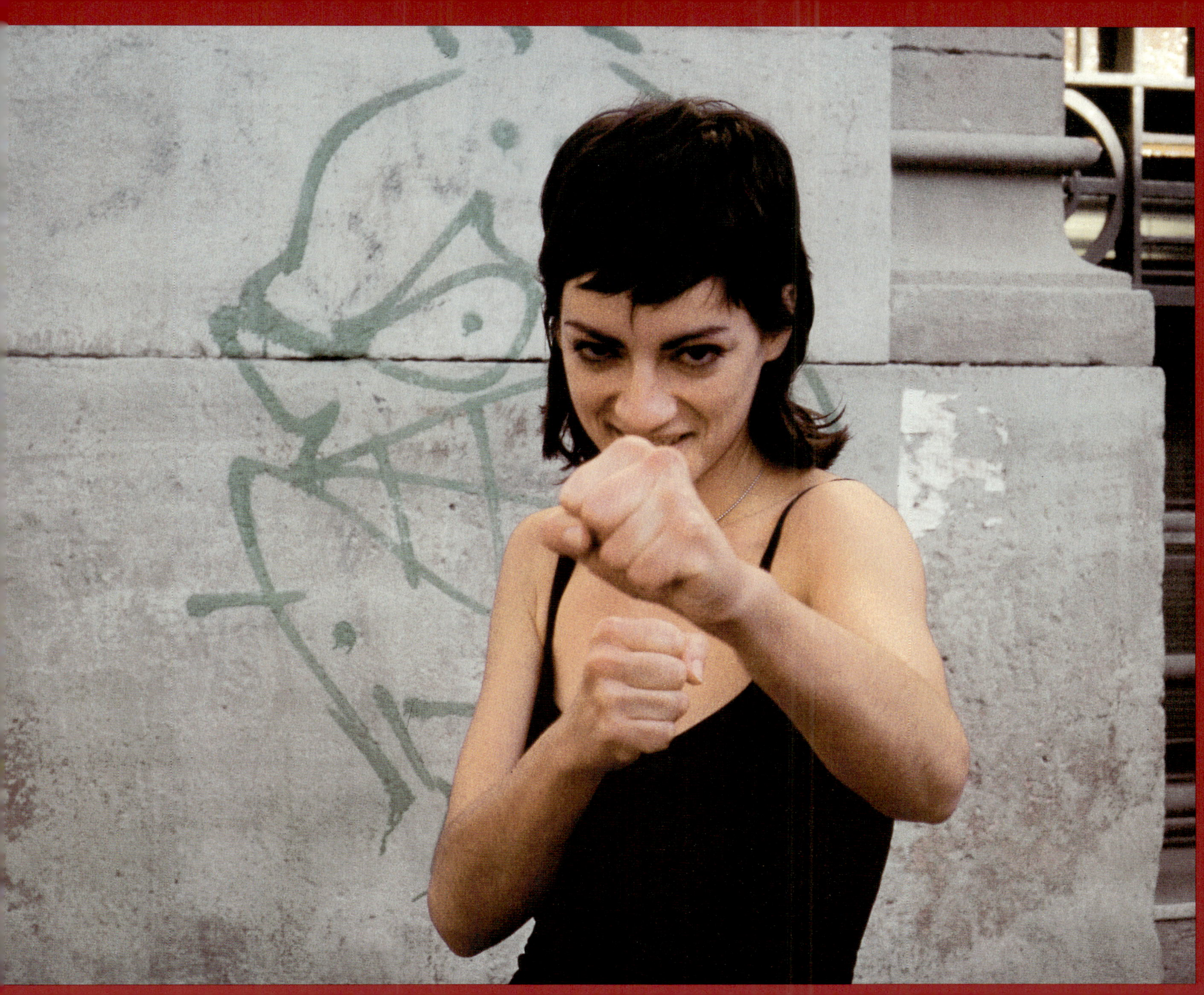

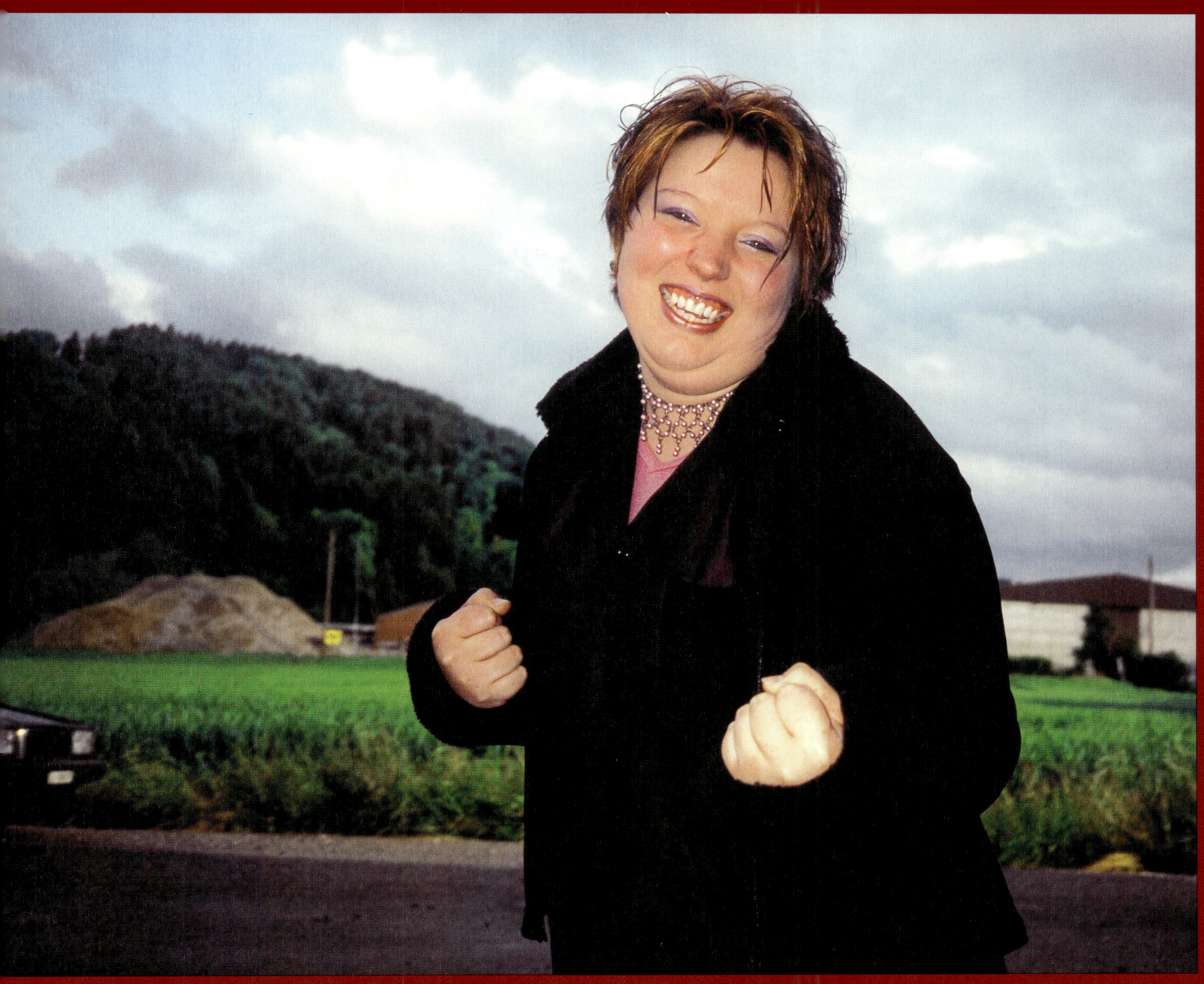

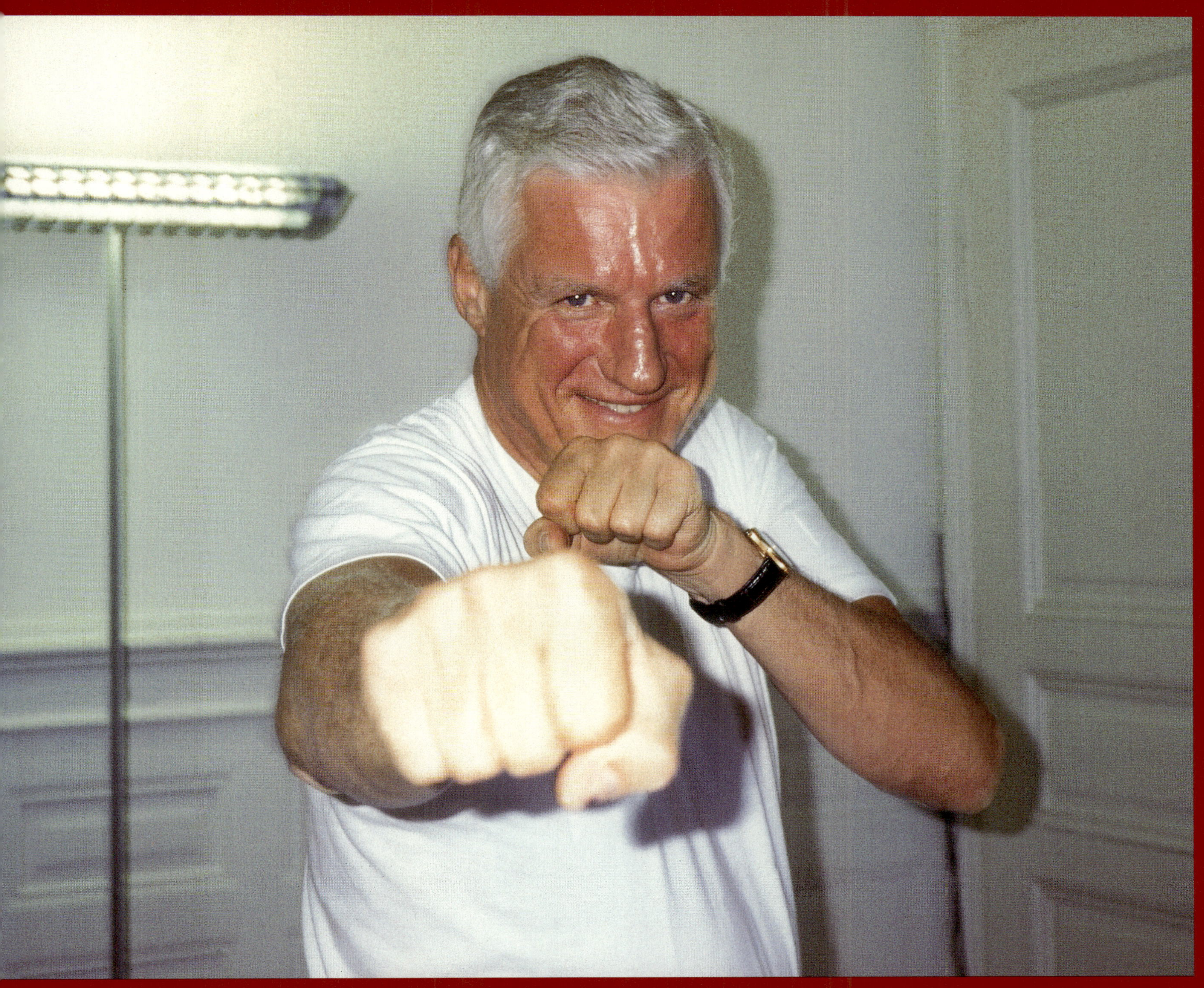

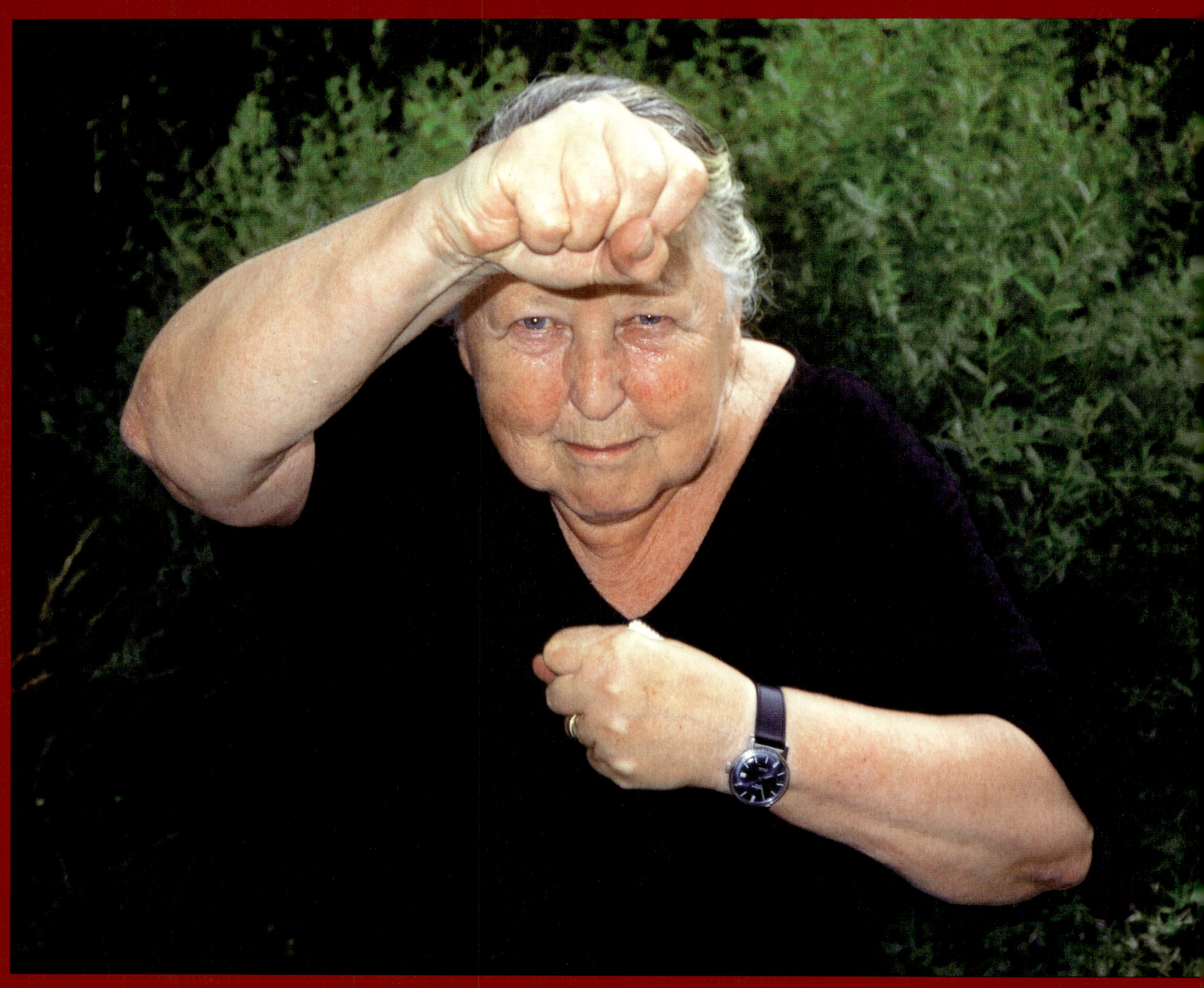

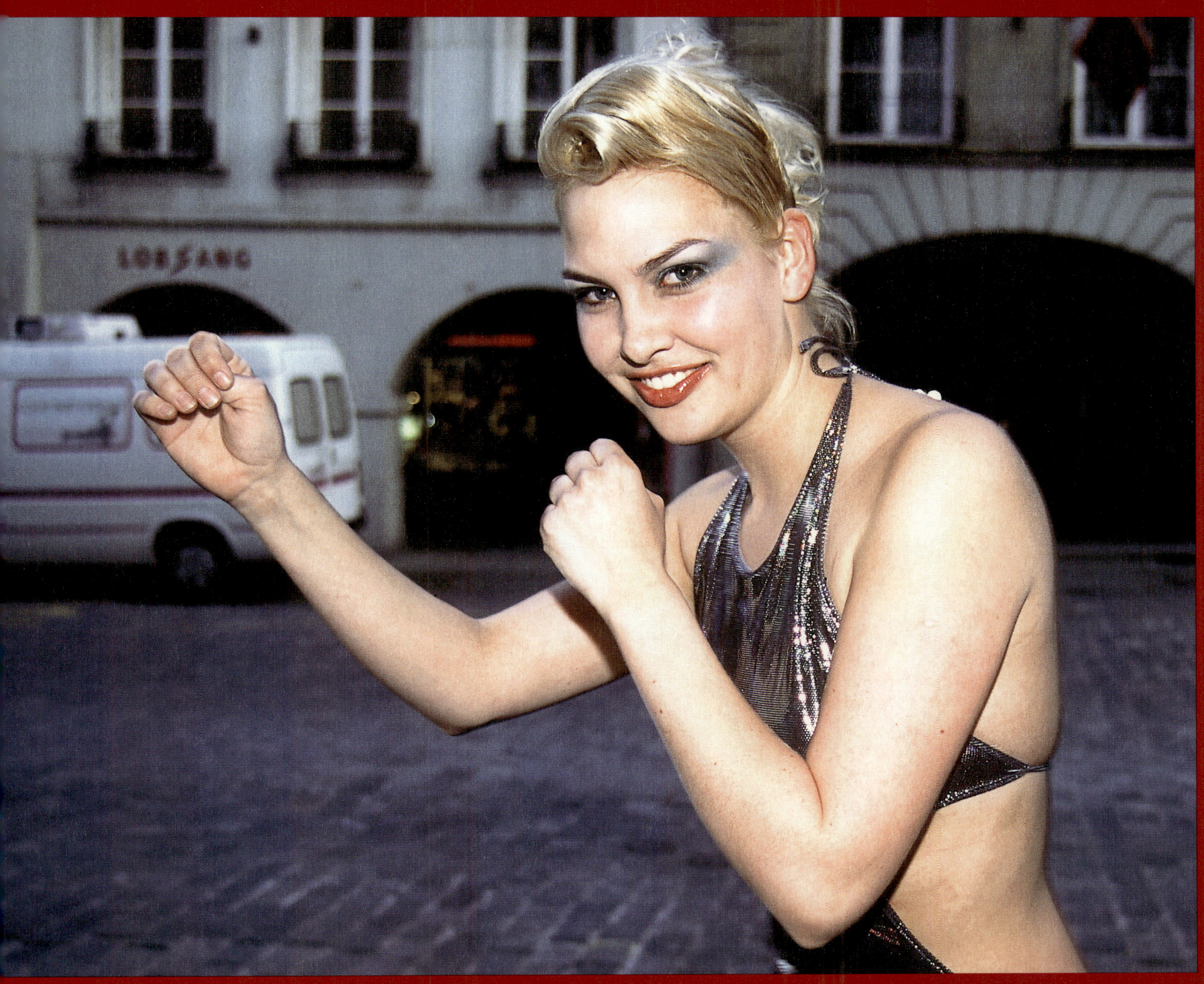
LOBSANG

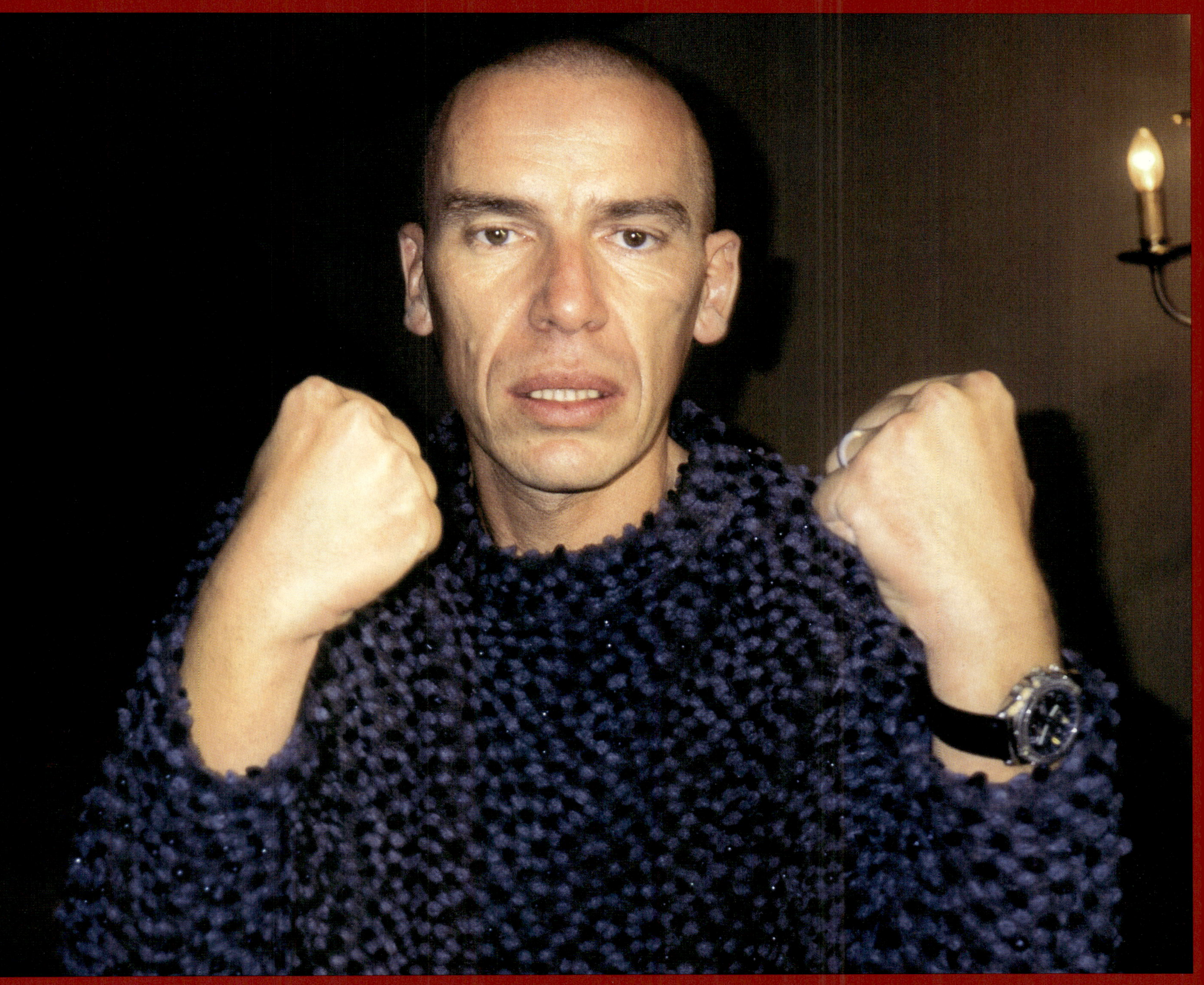

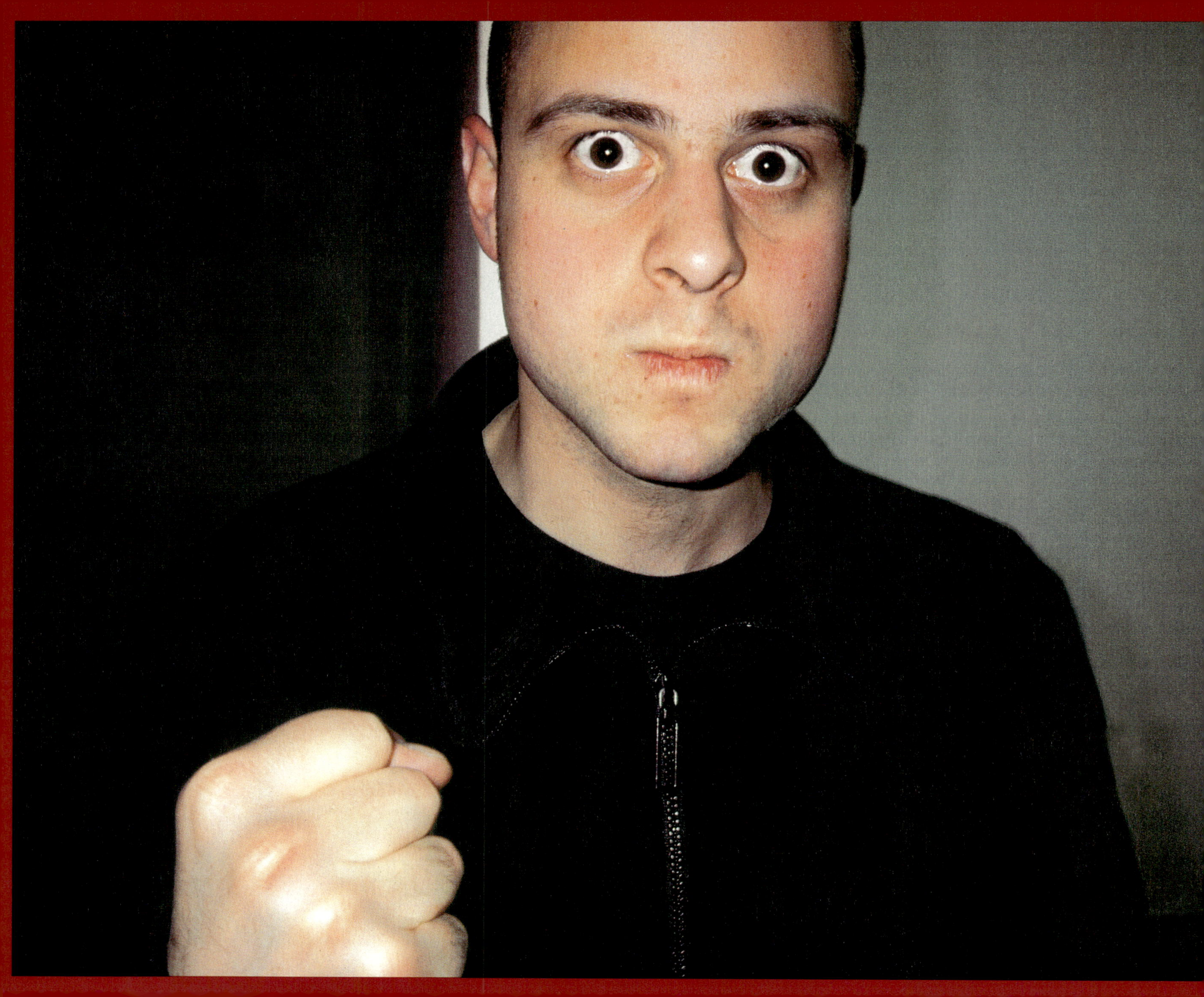

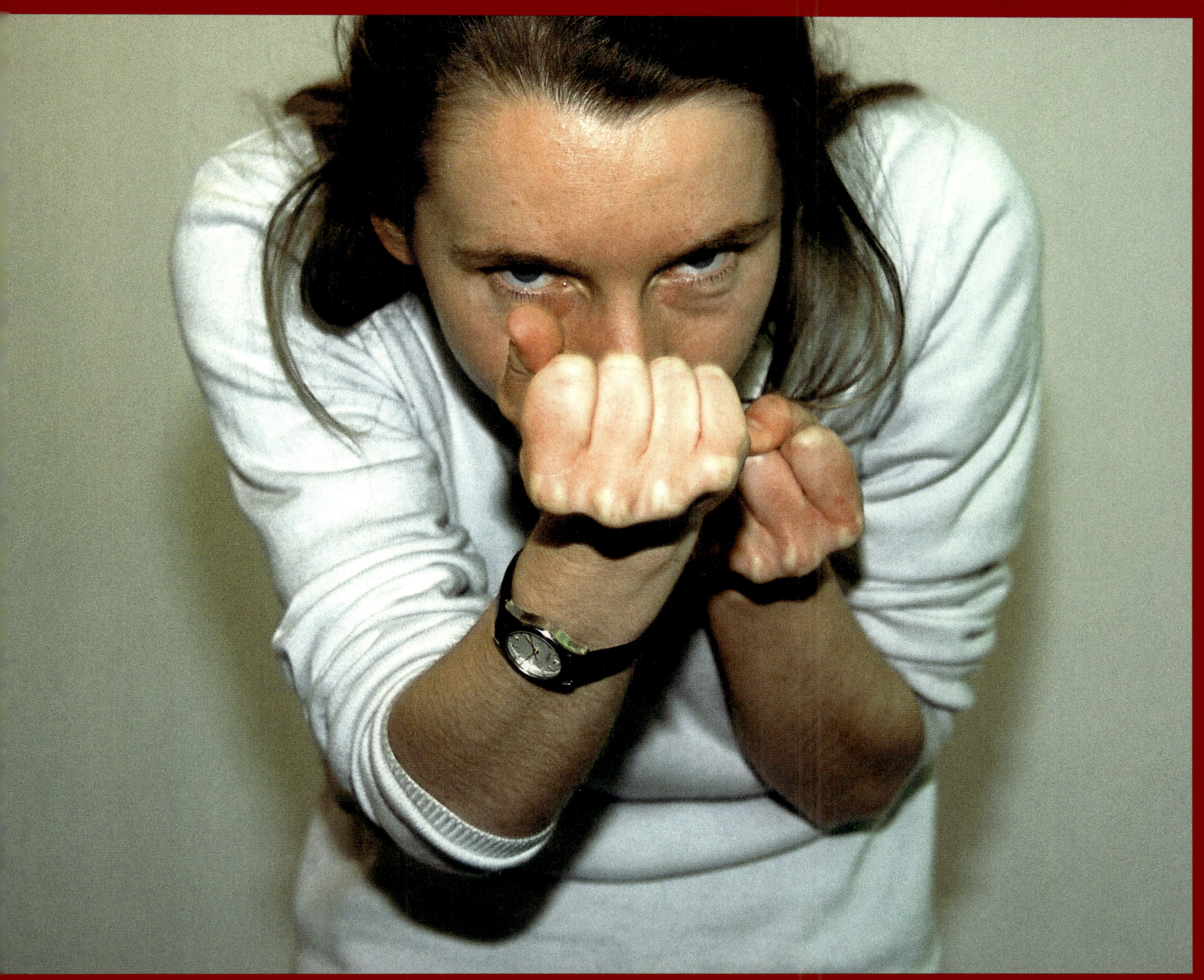

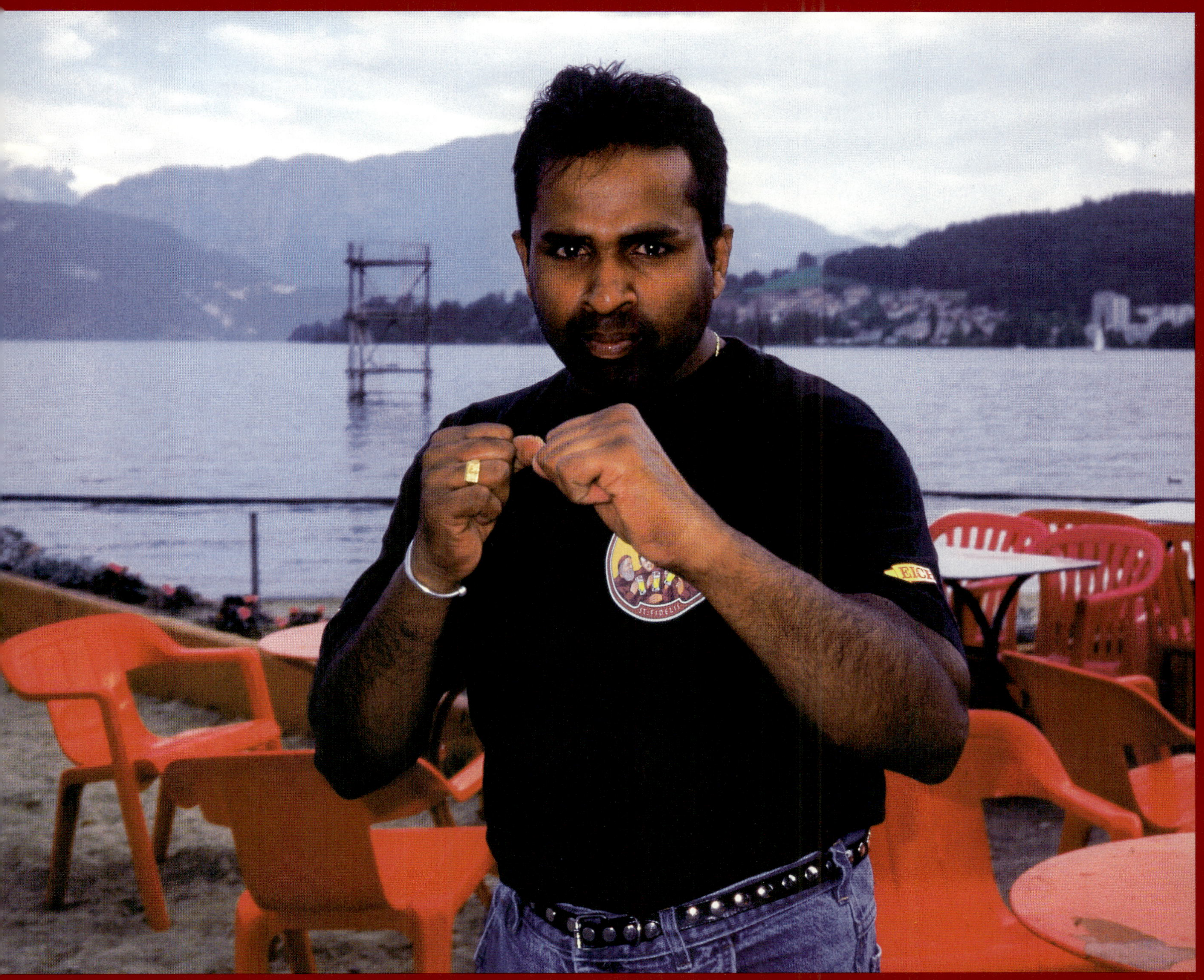

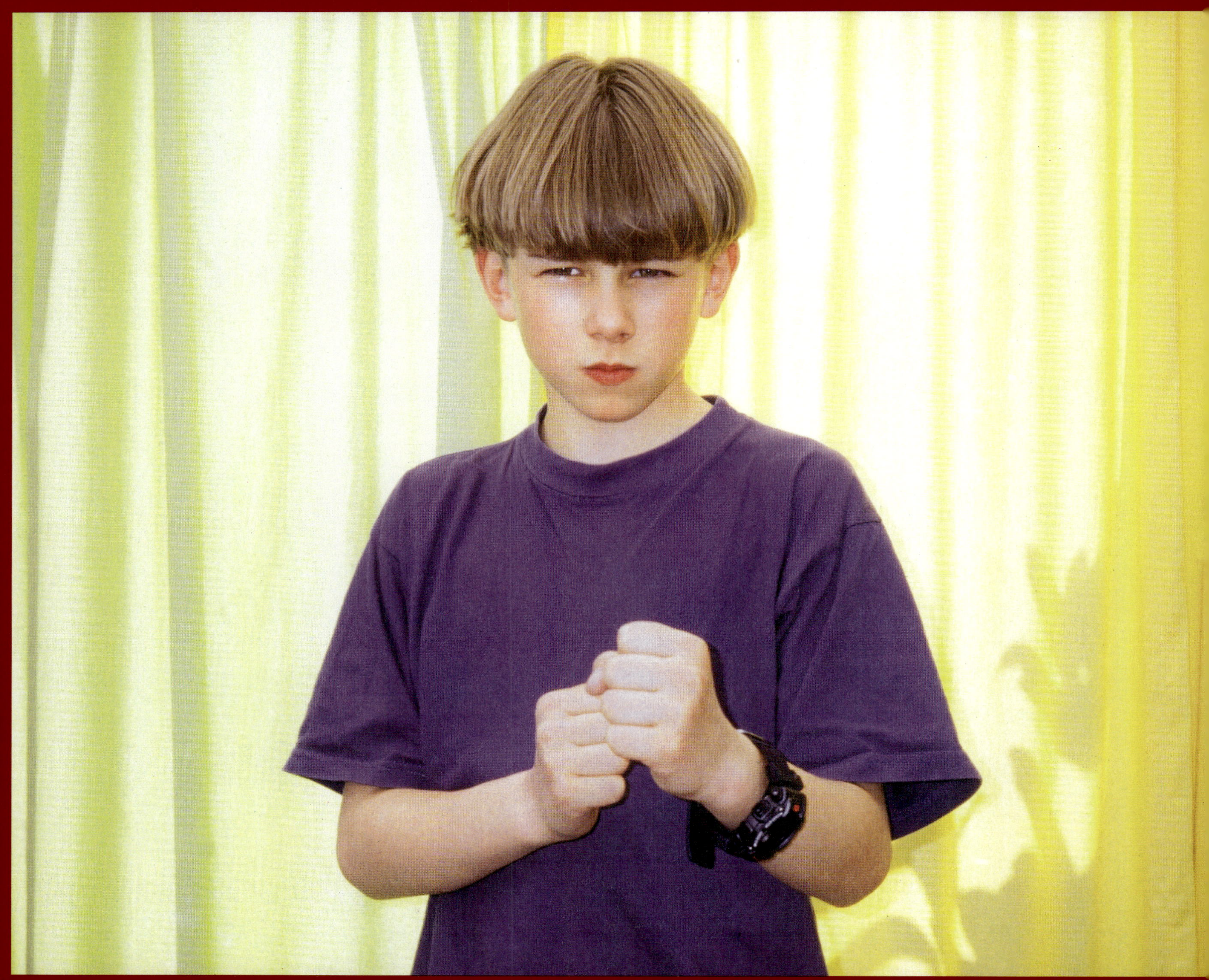

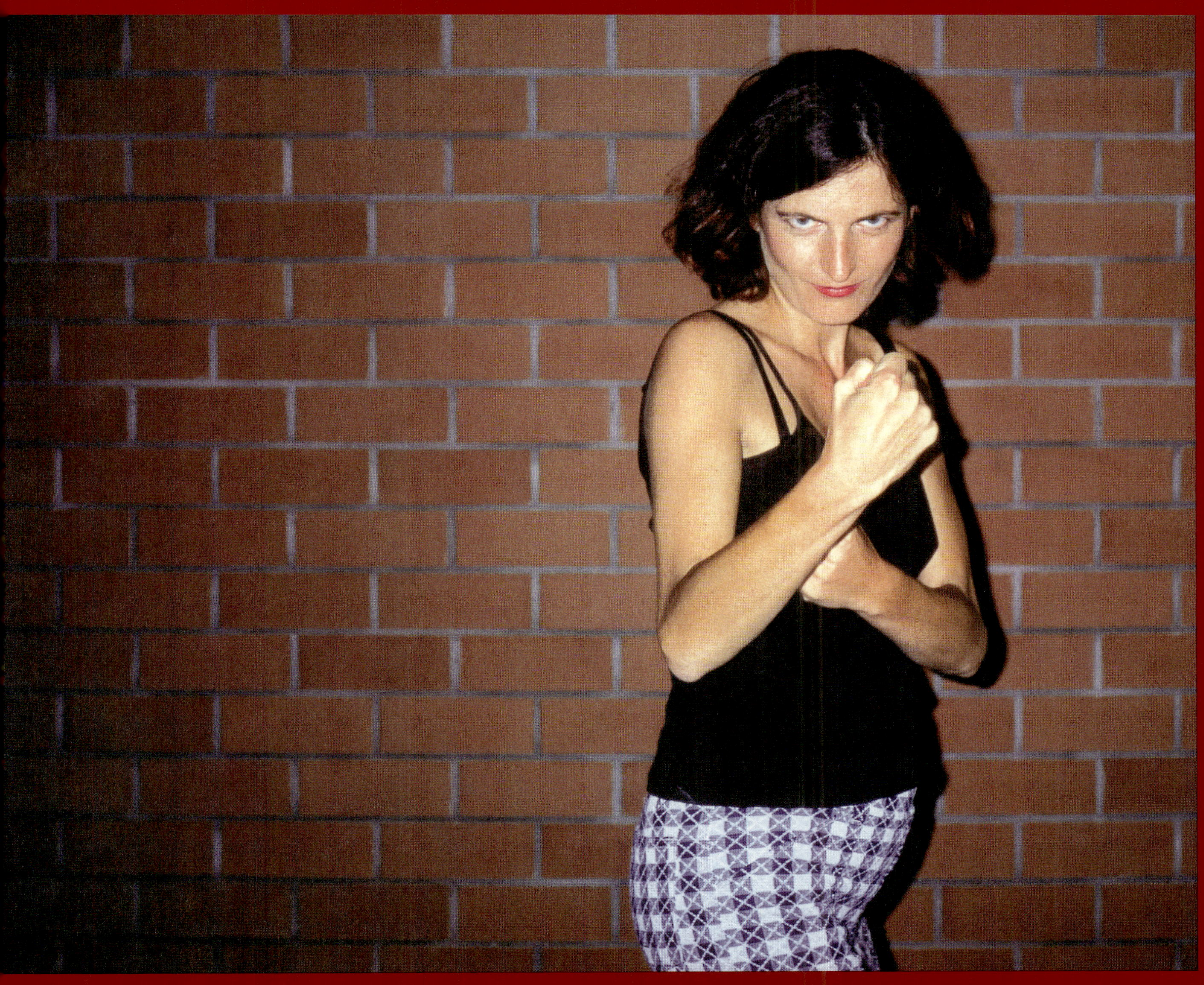

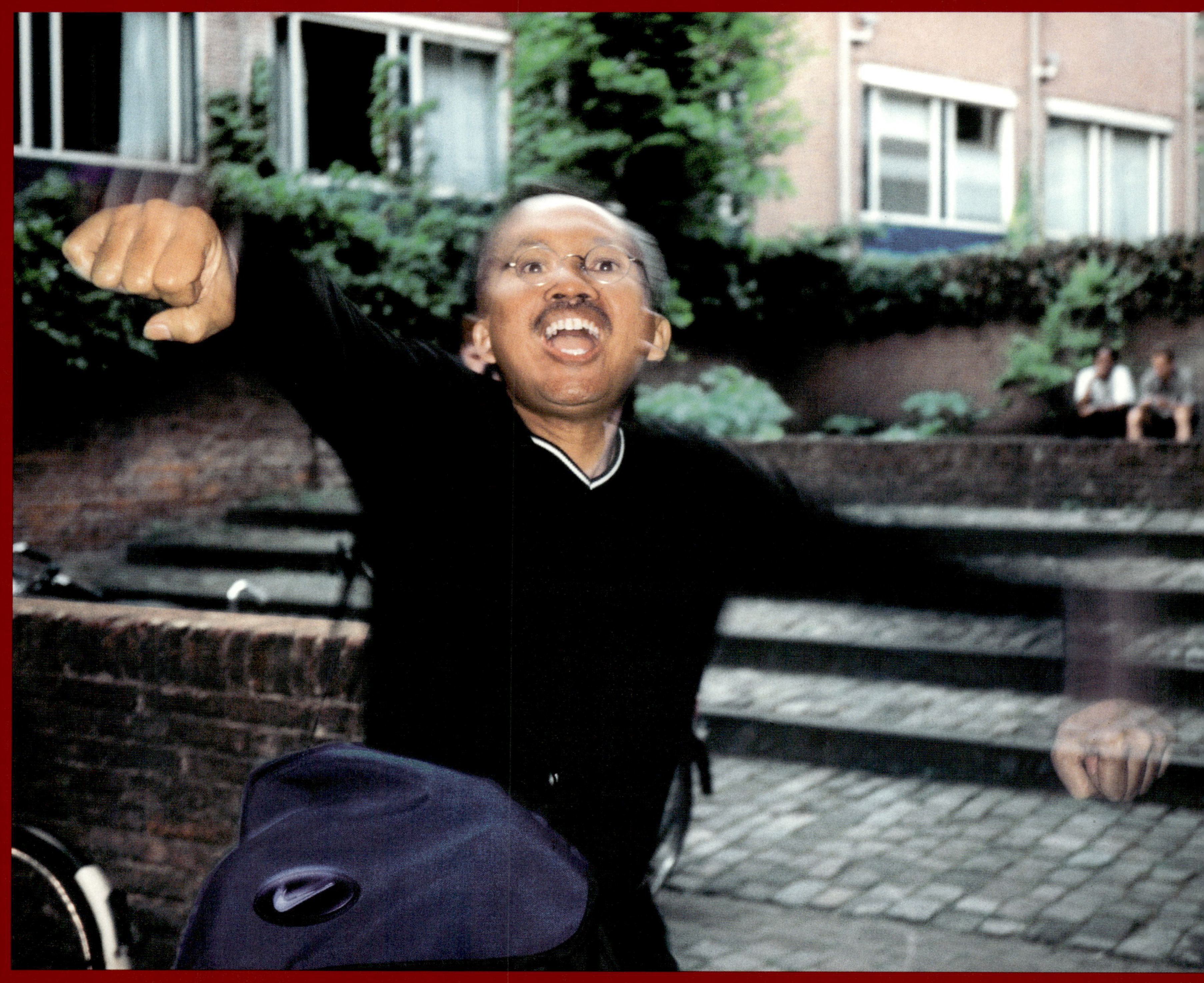

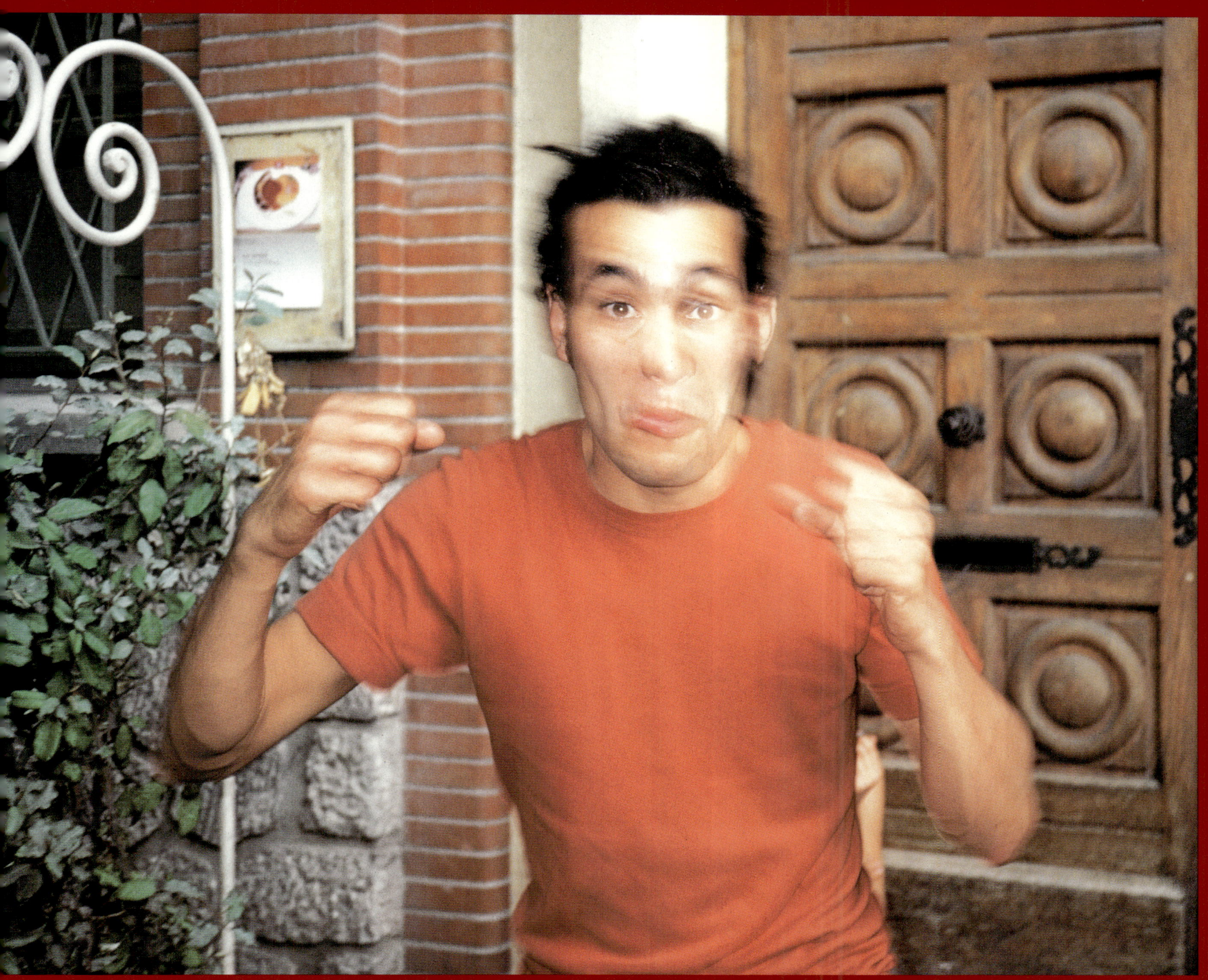

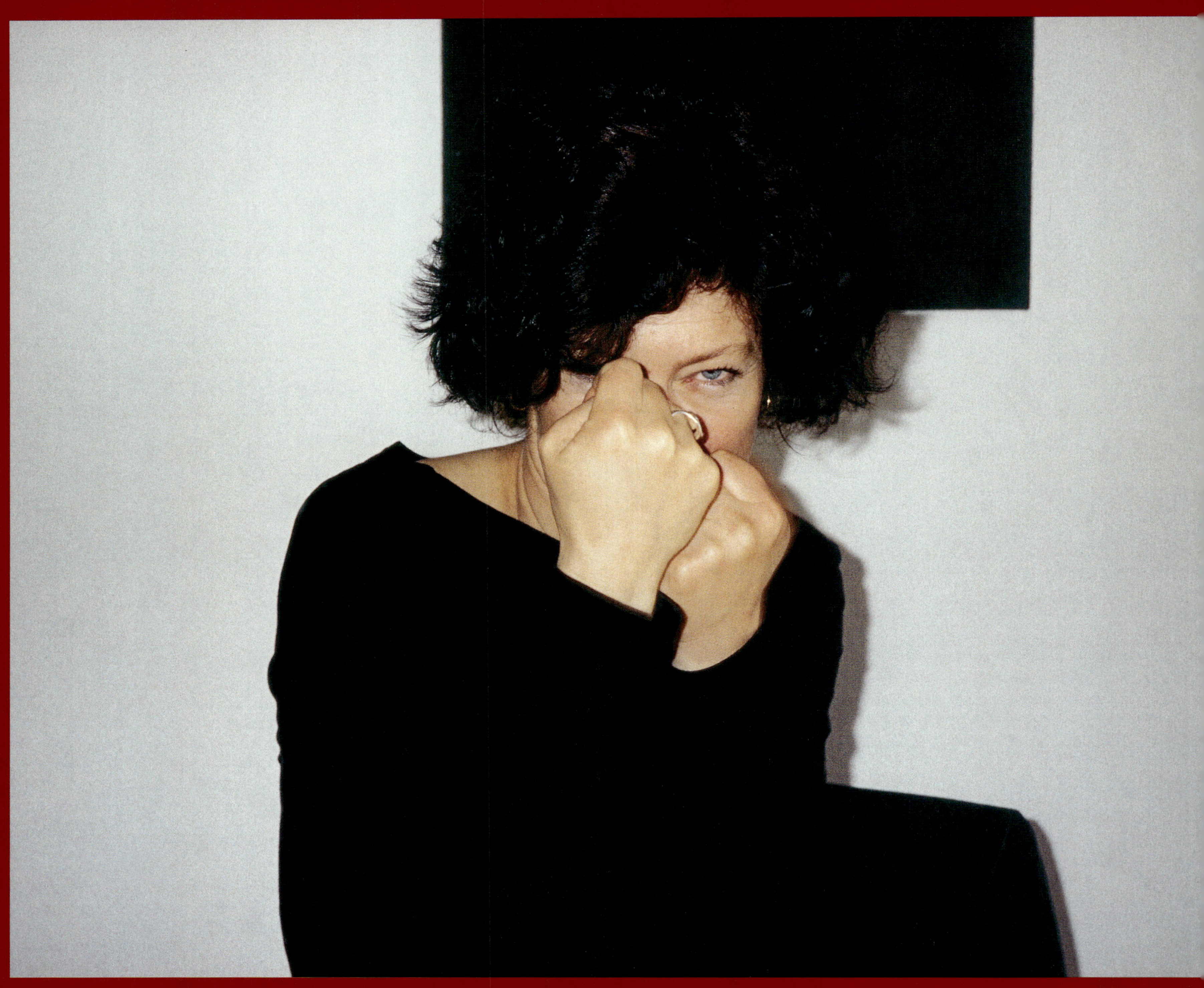

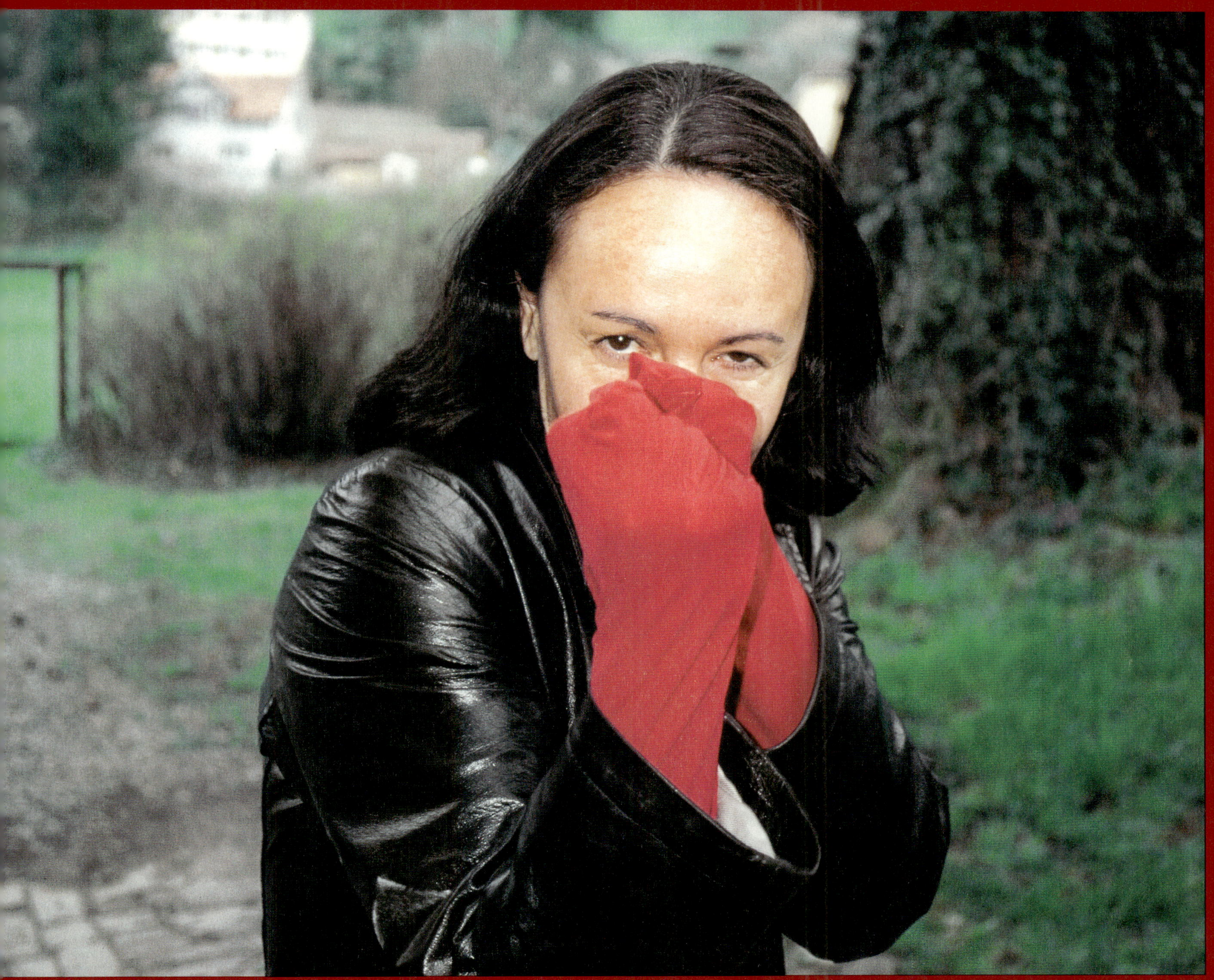

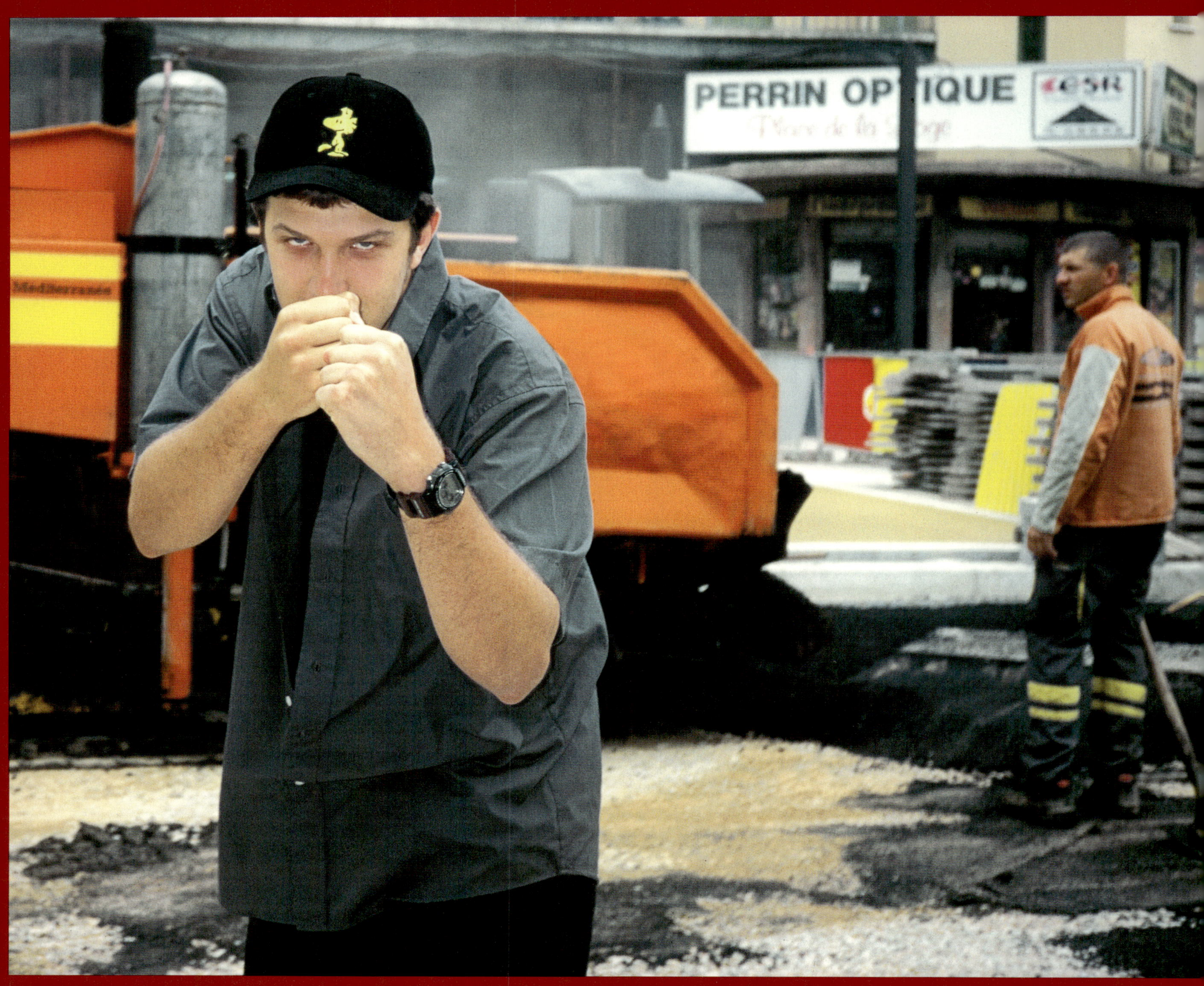
PERRIN OPTIQUE

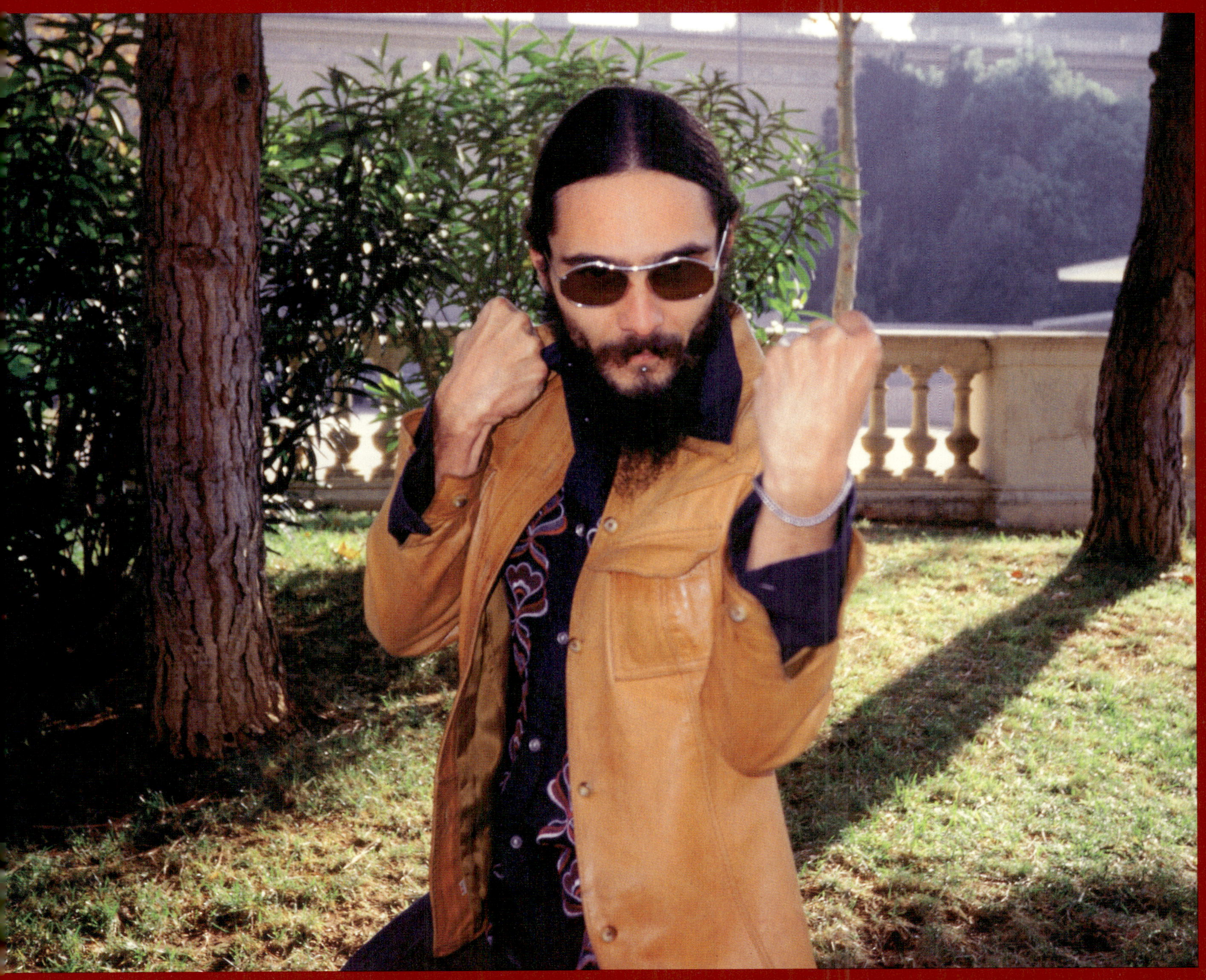

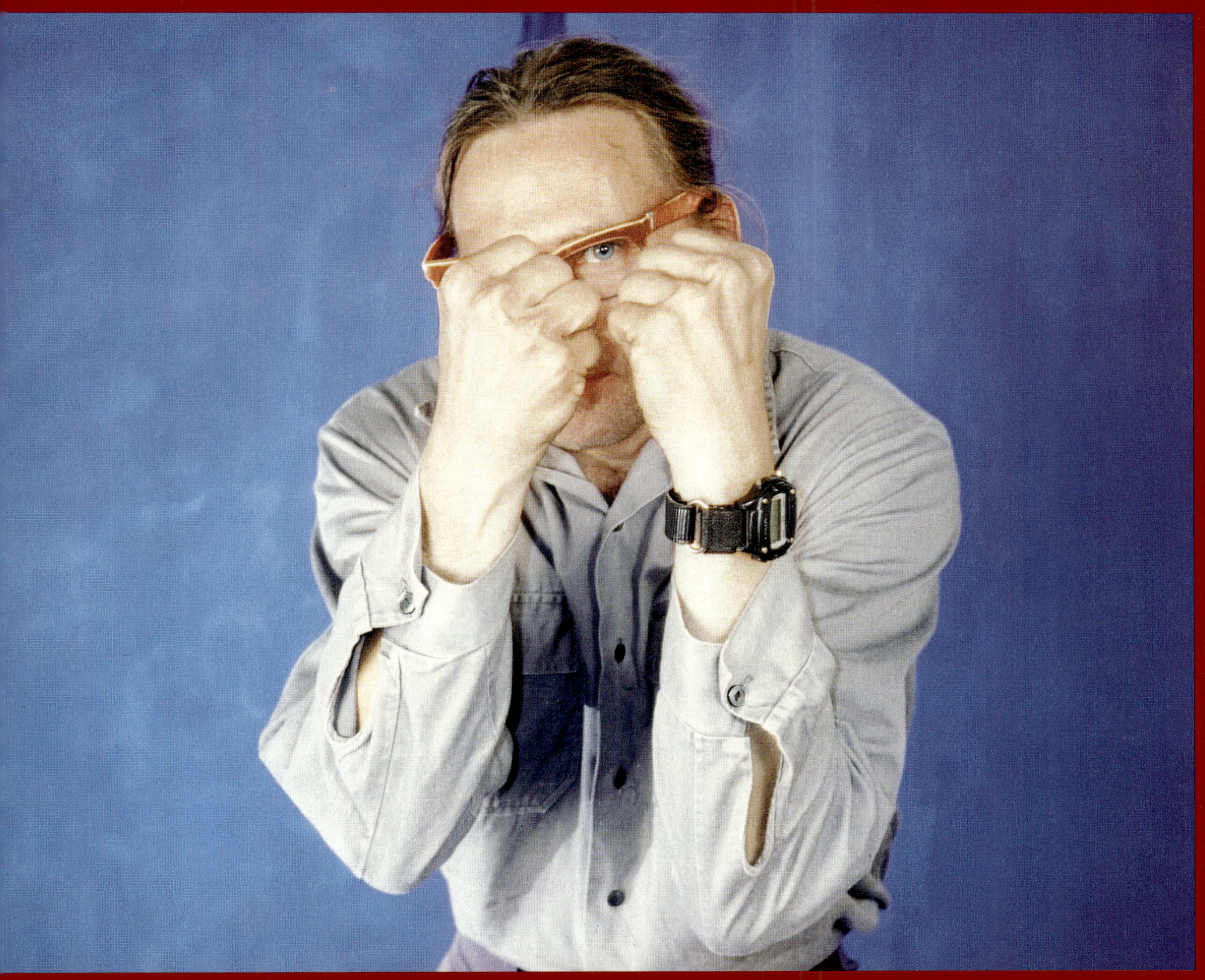

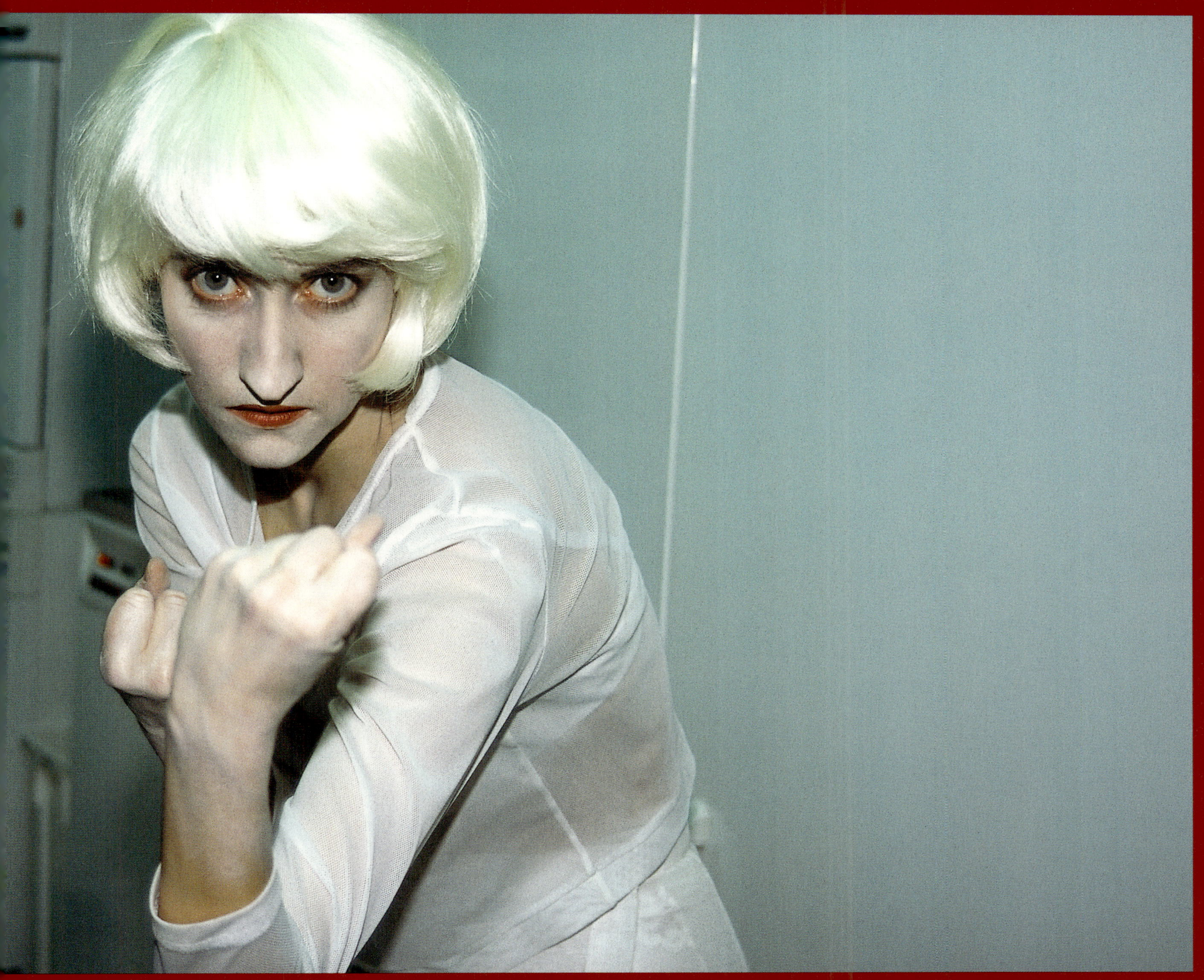

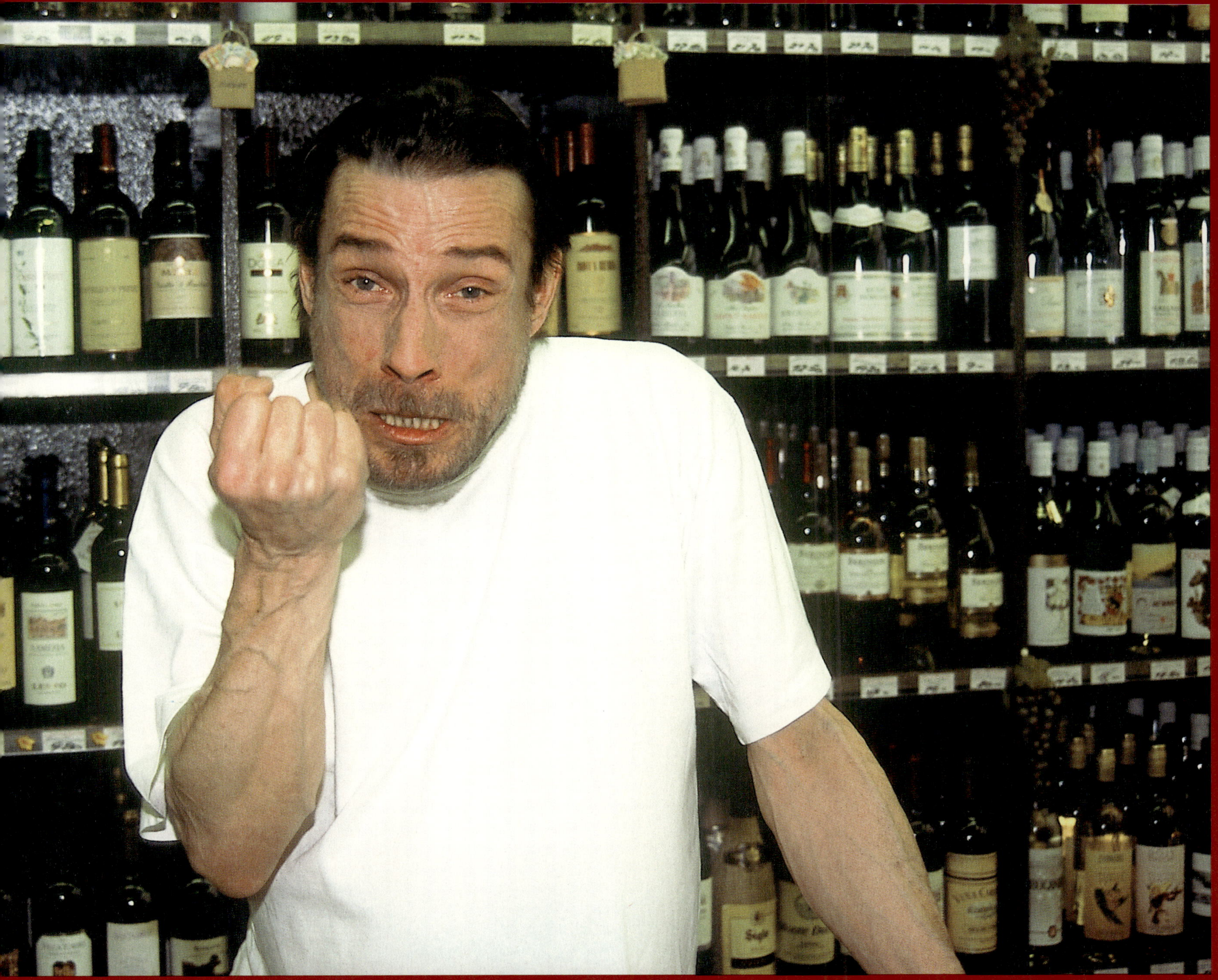

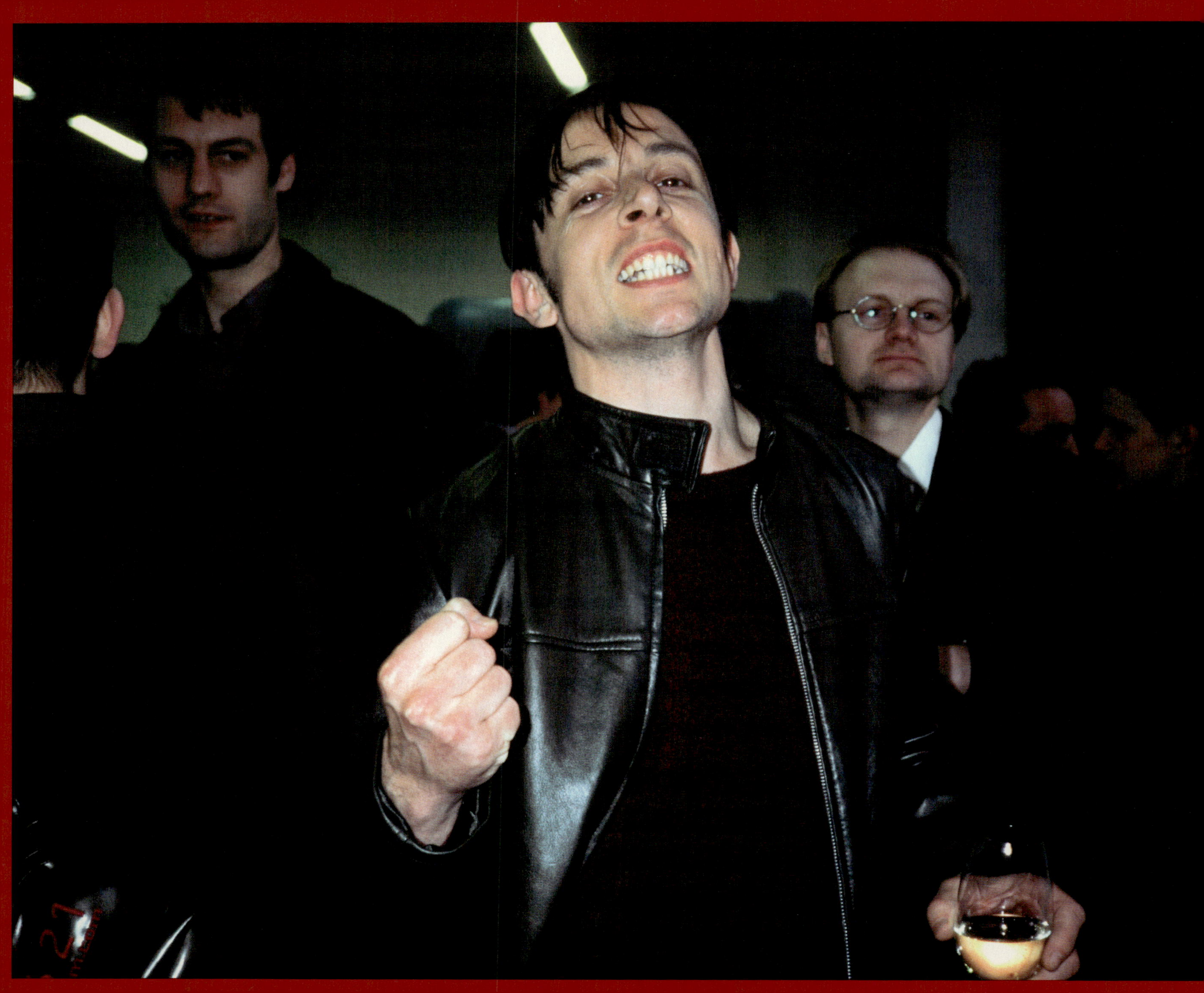

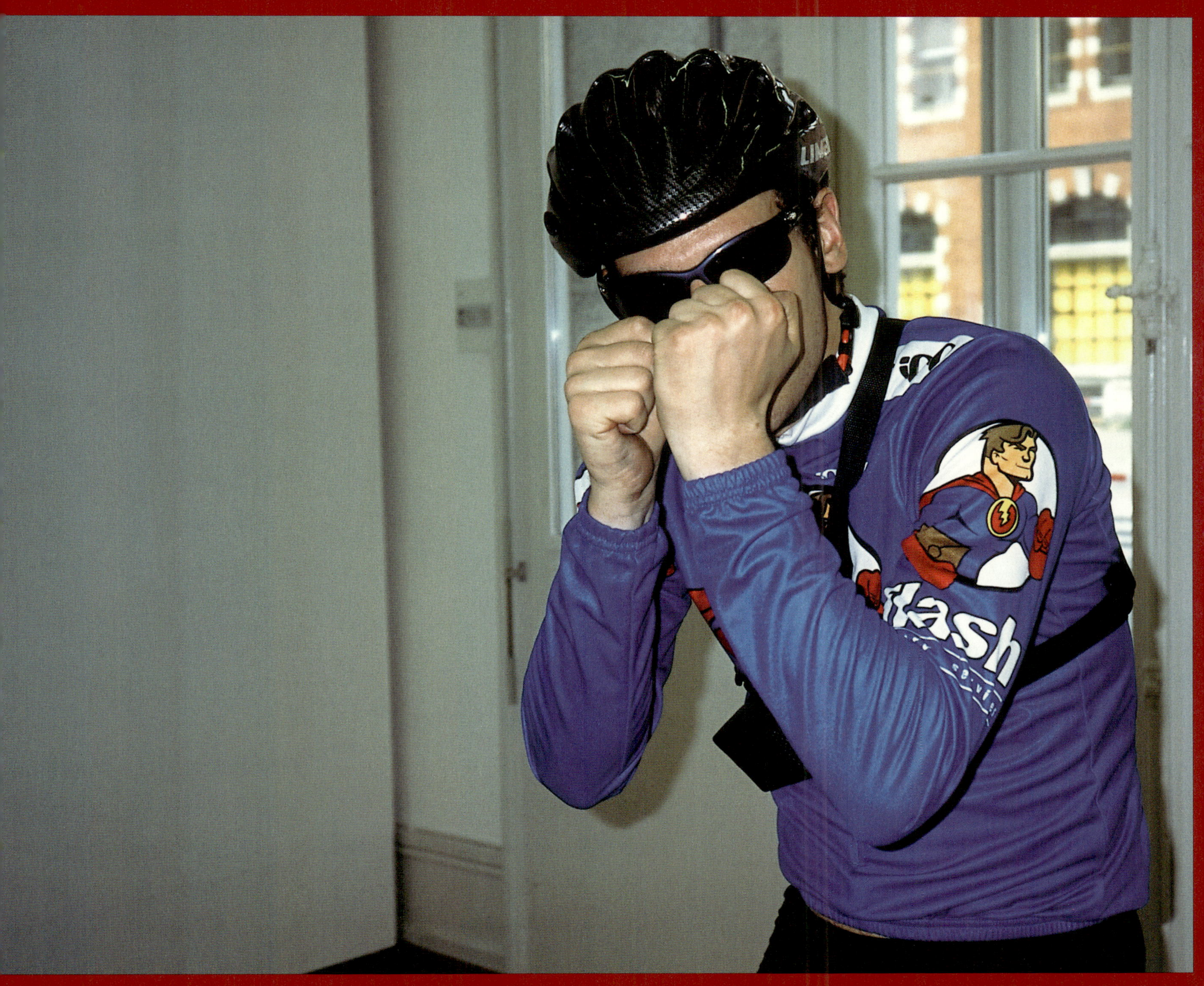

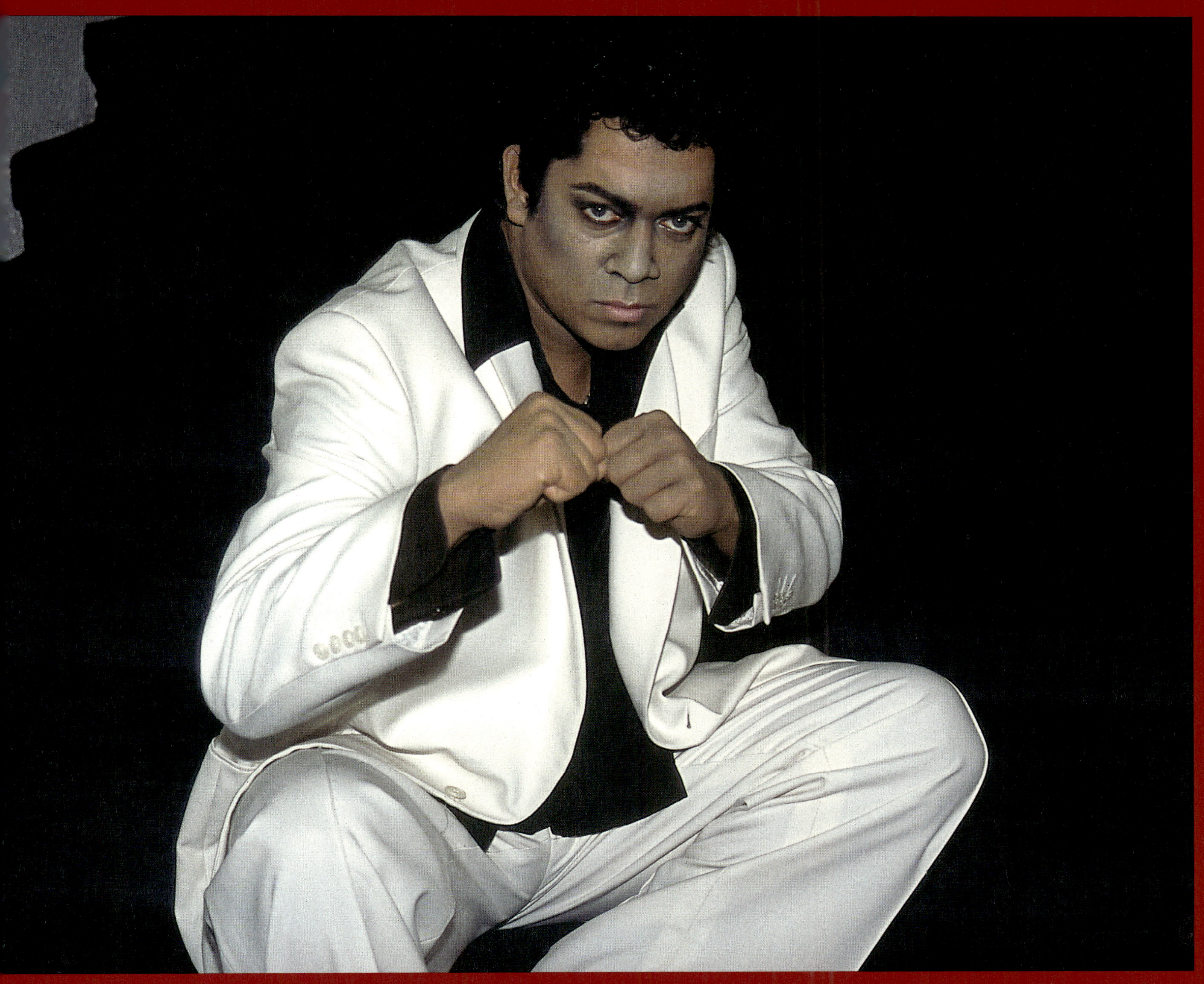

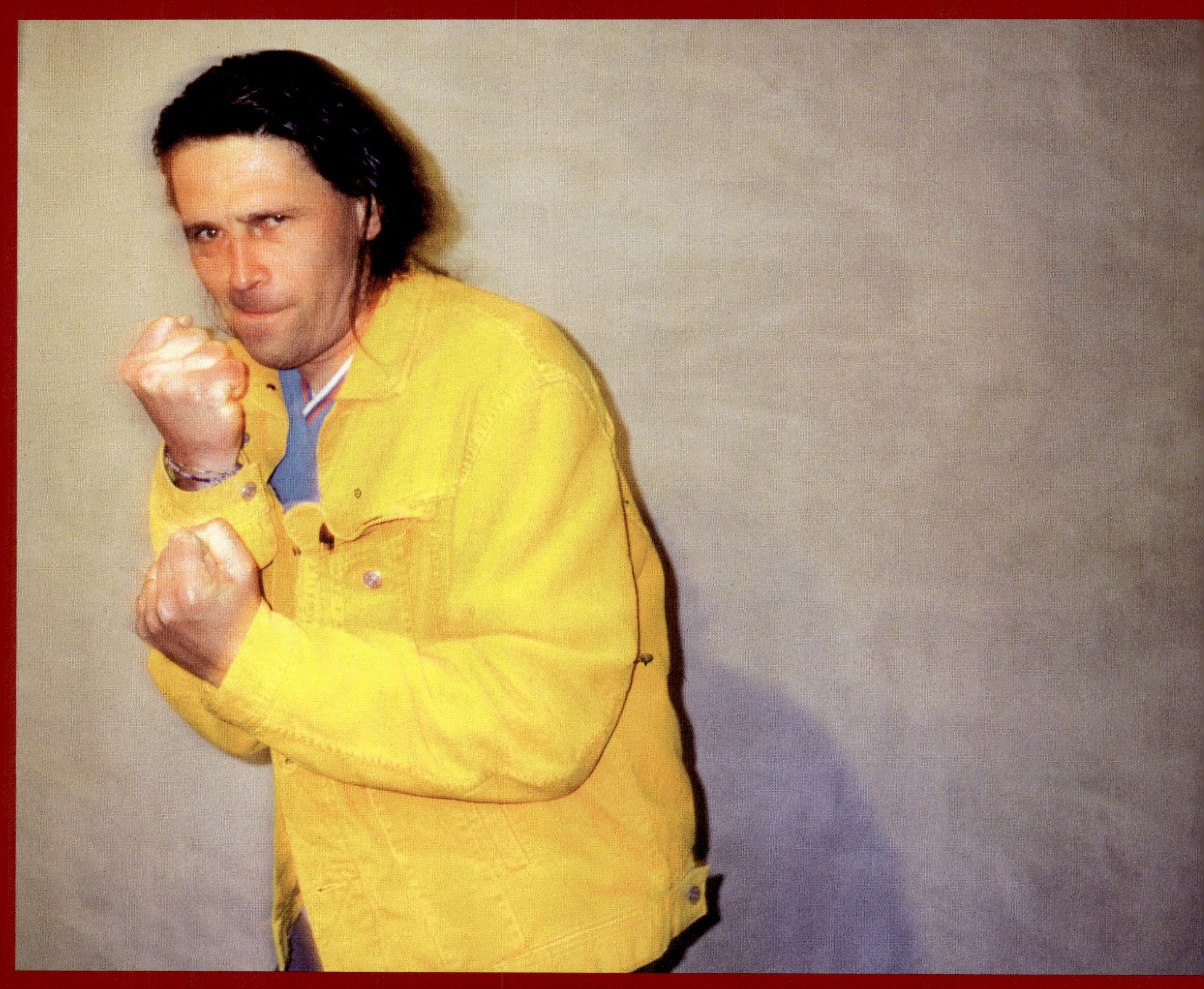

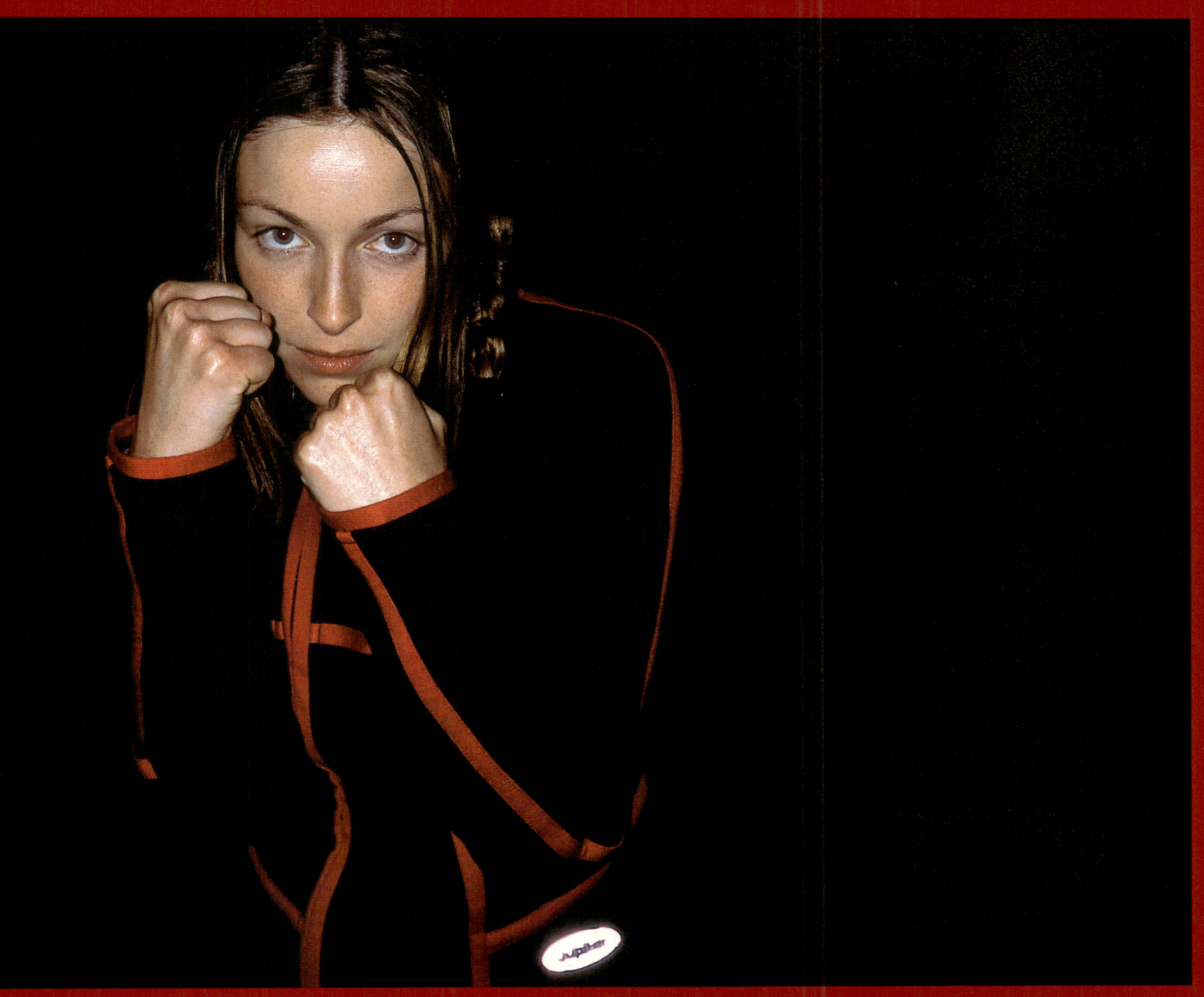

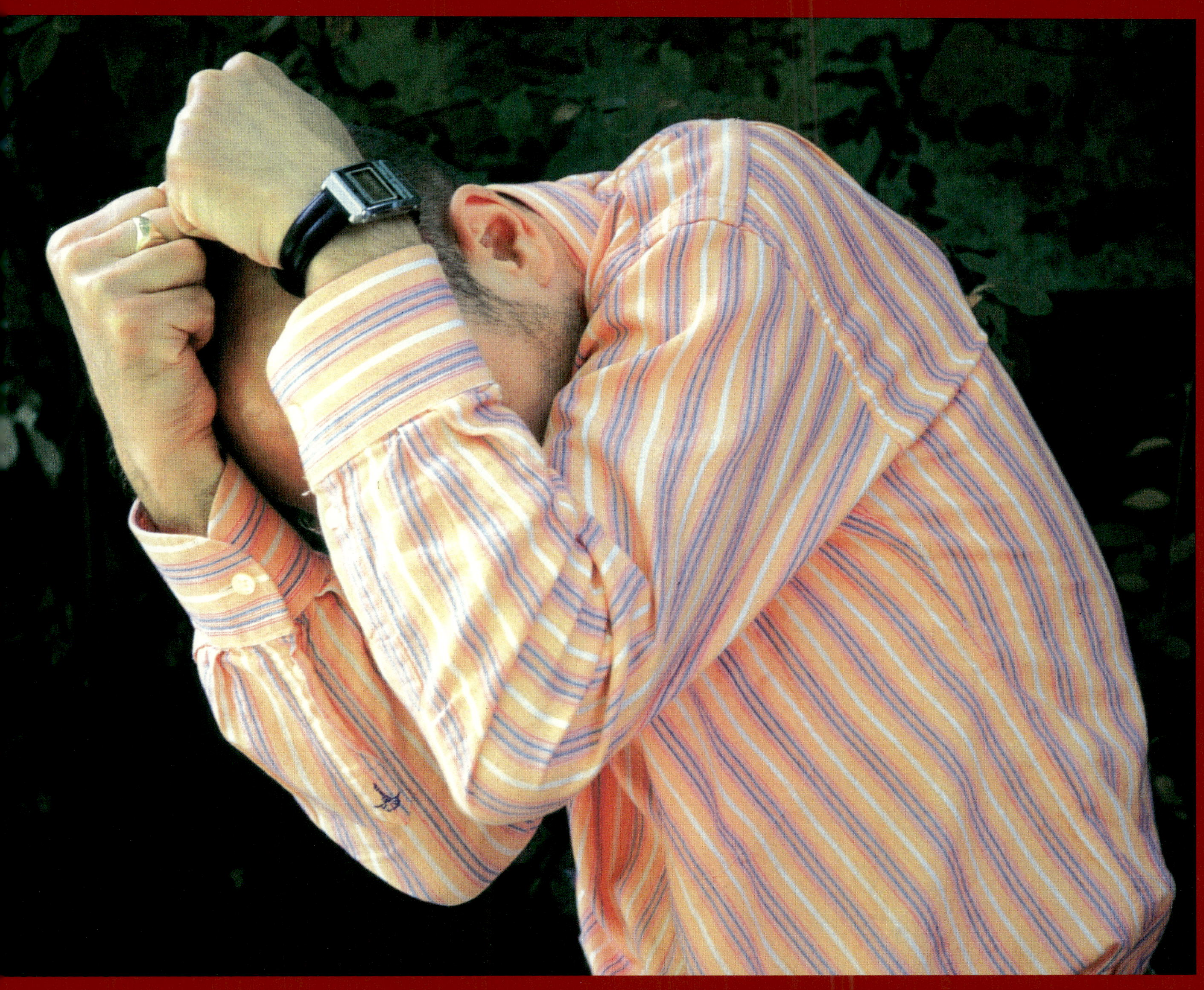

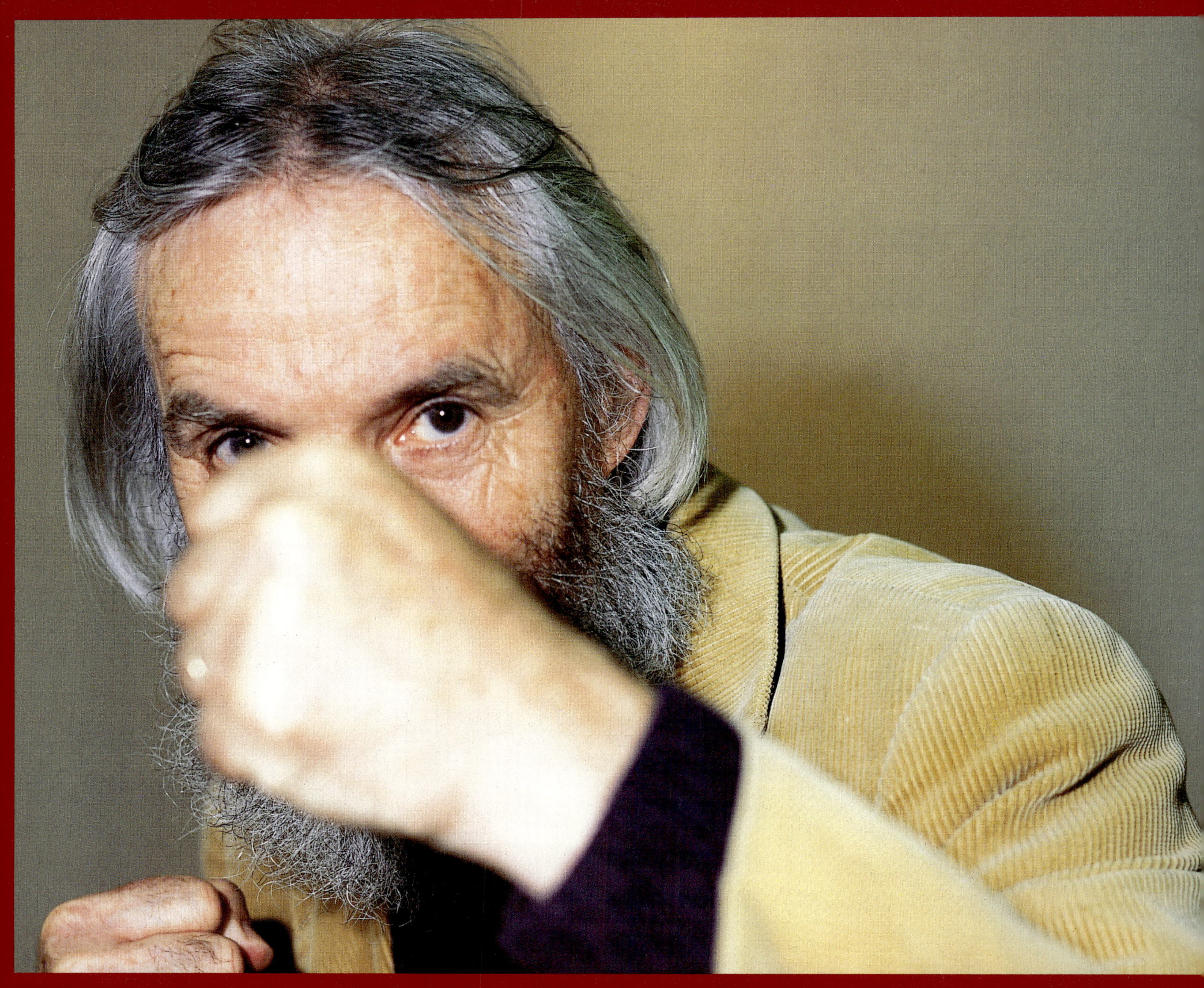

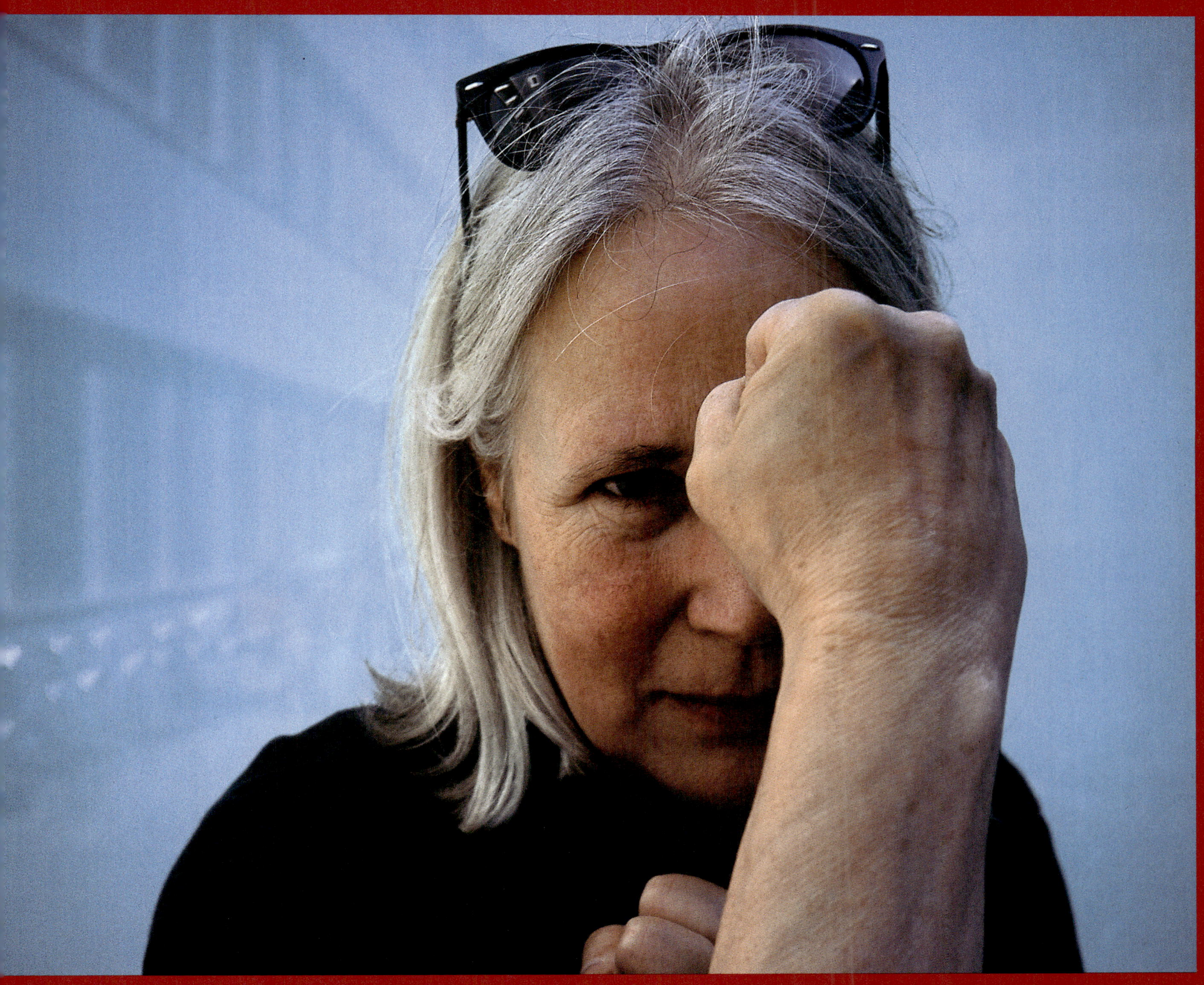

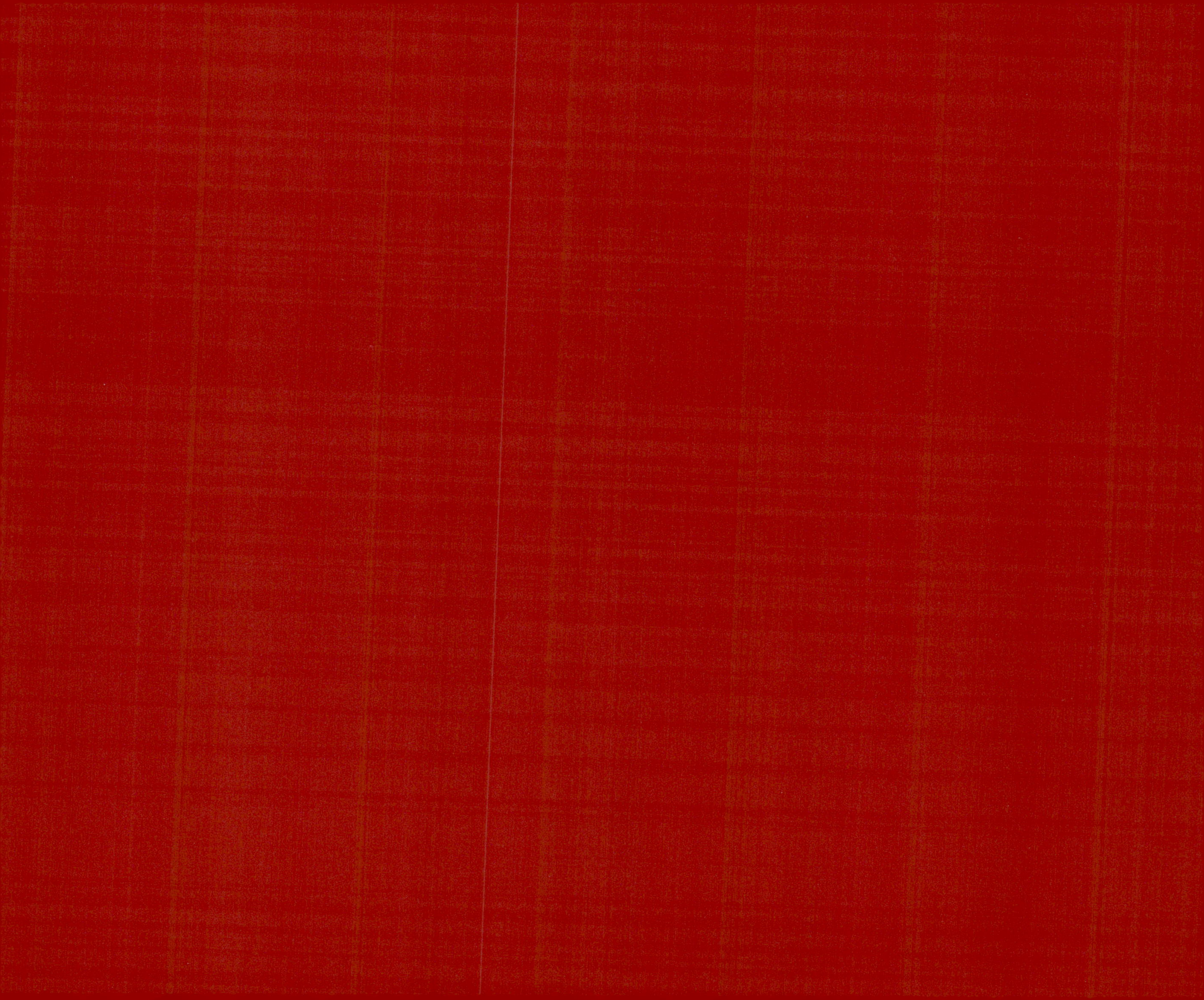

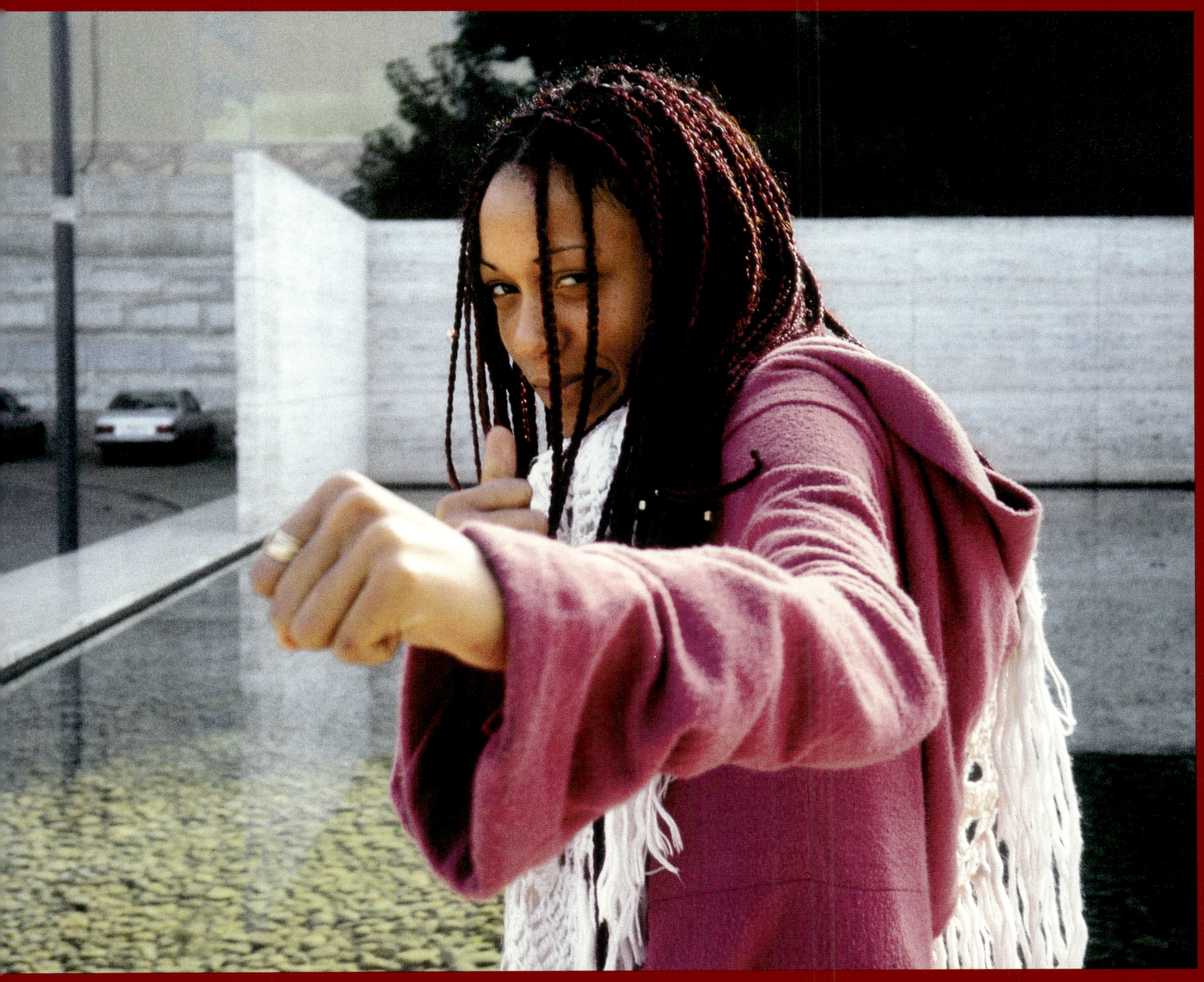

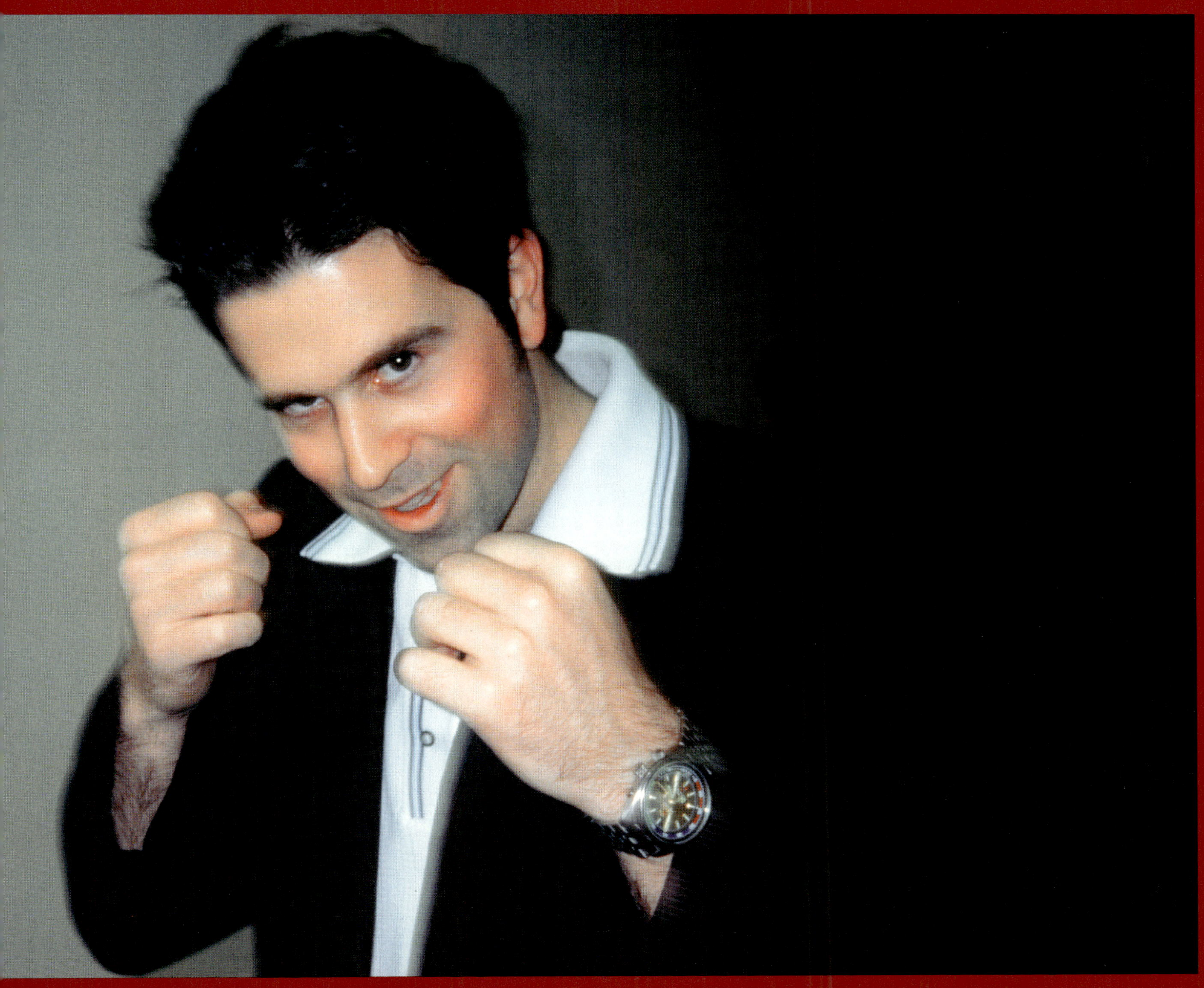

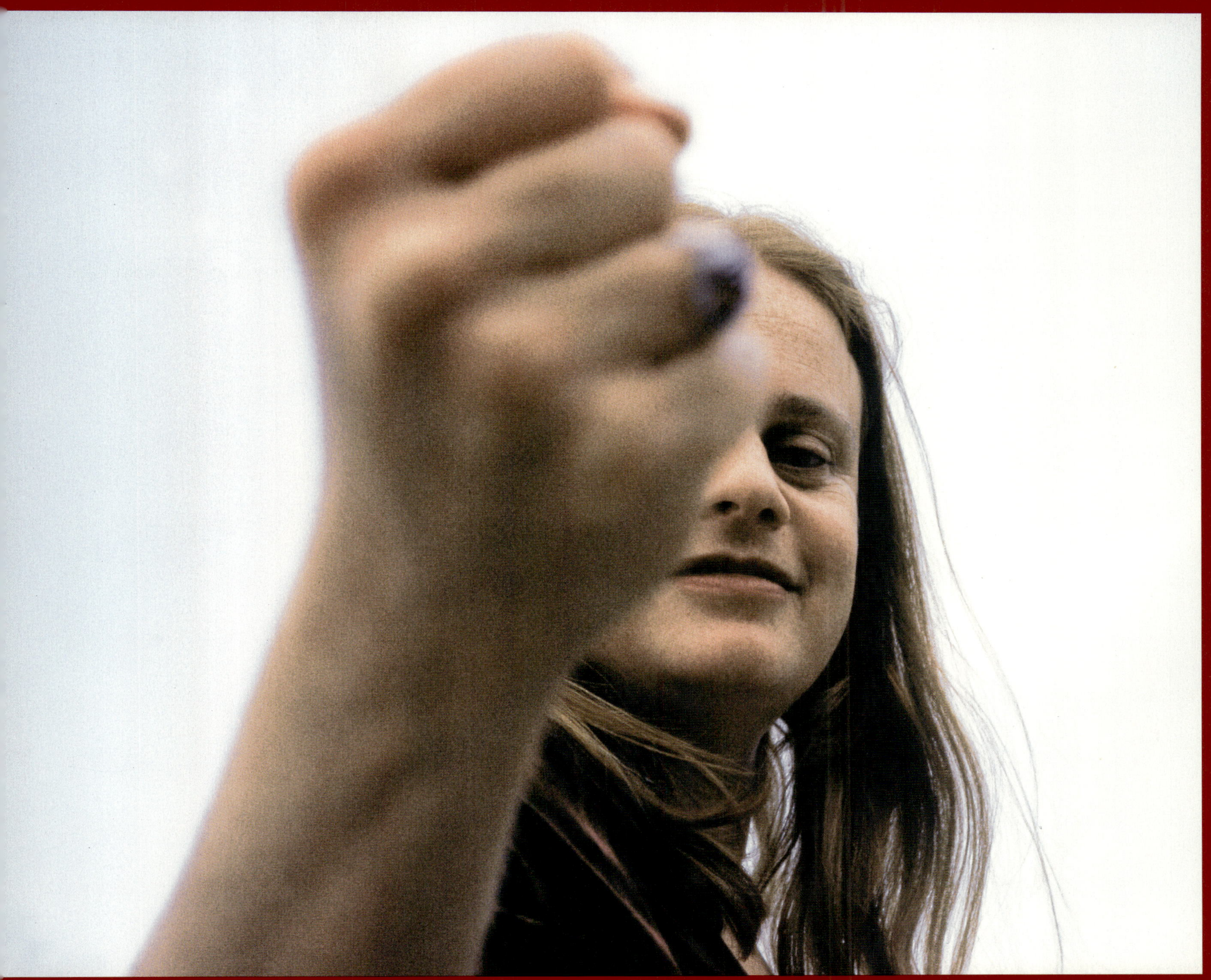

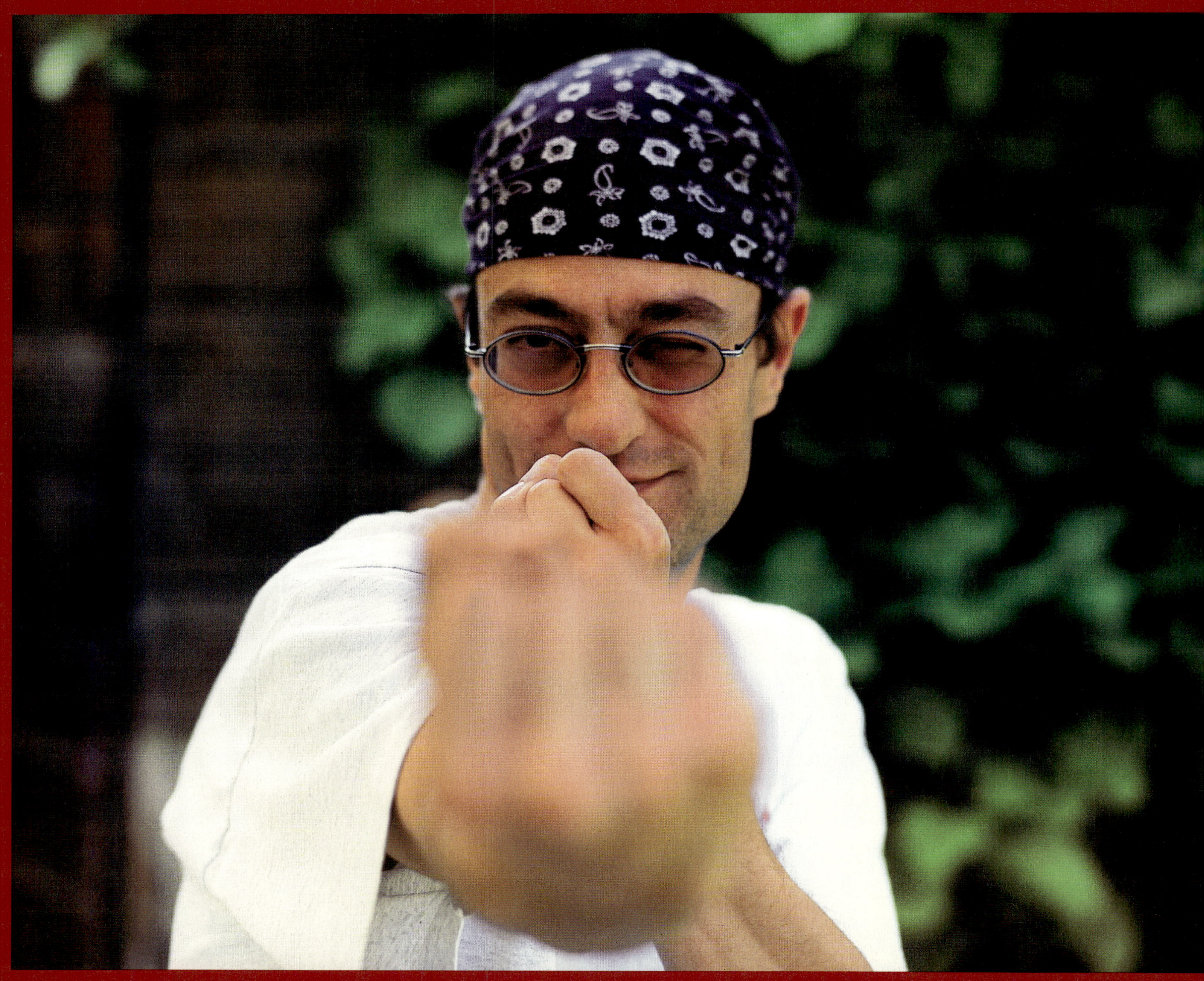

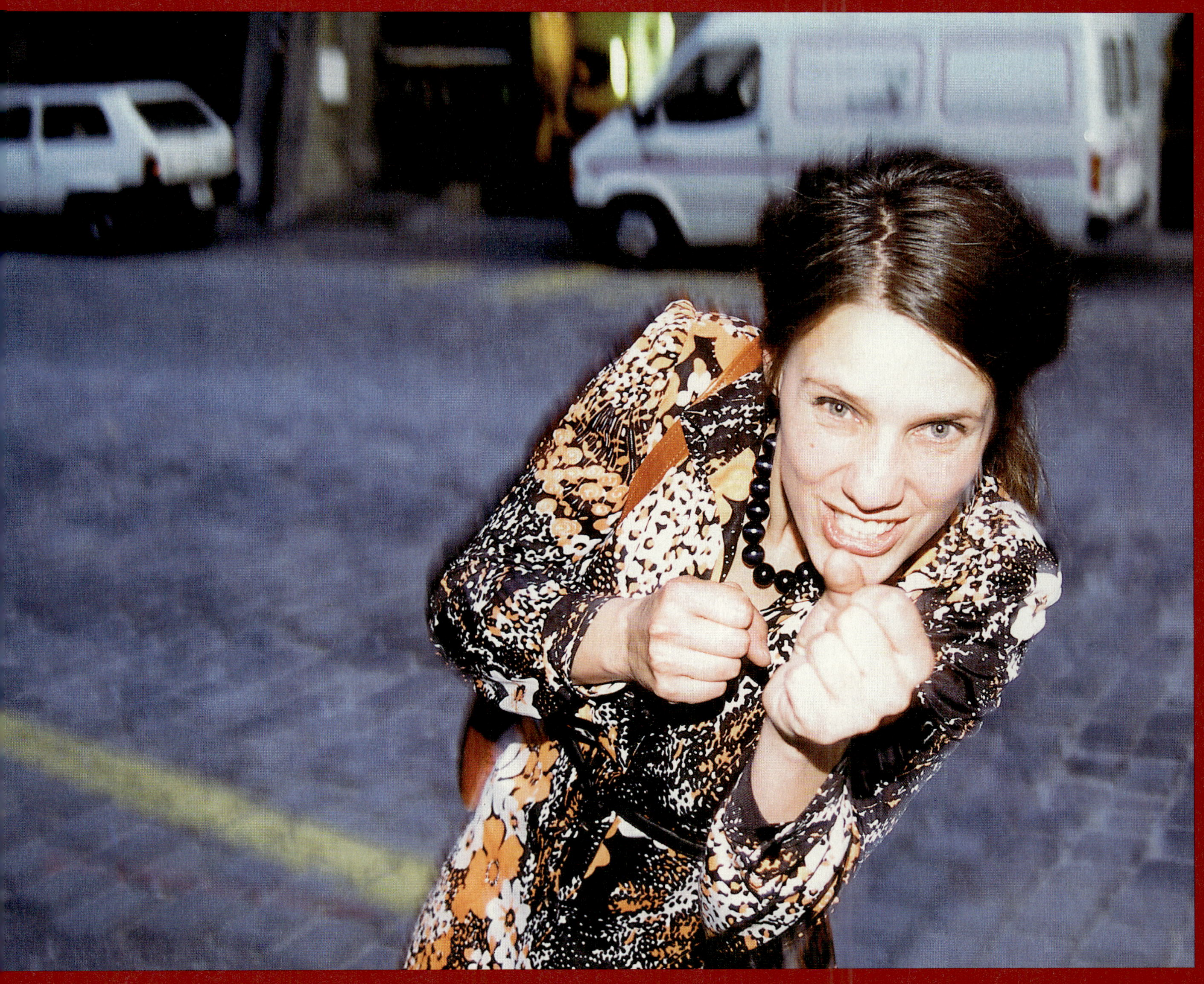

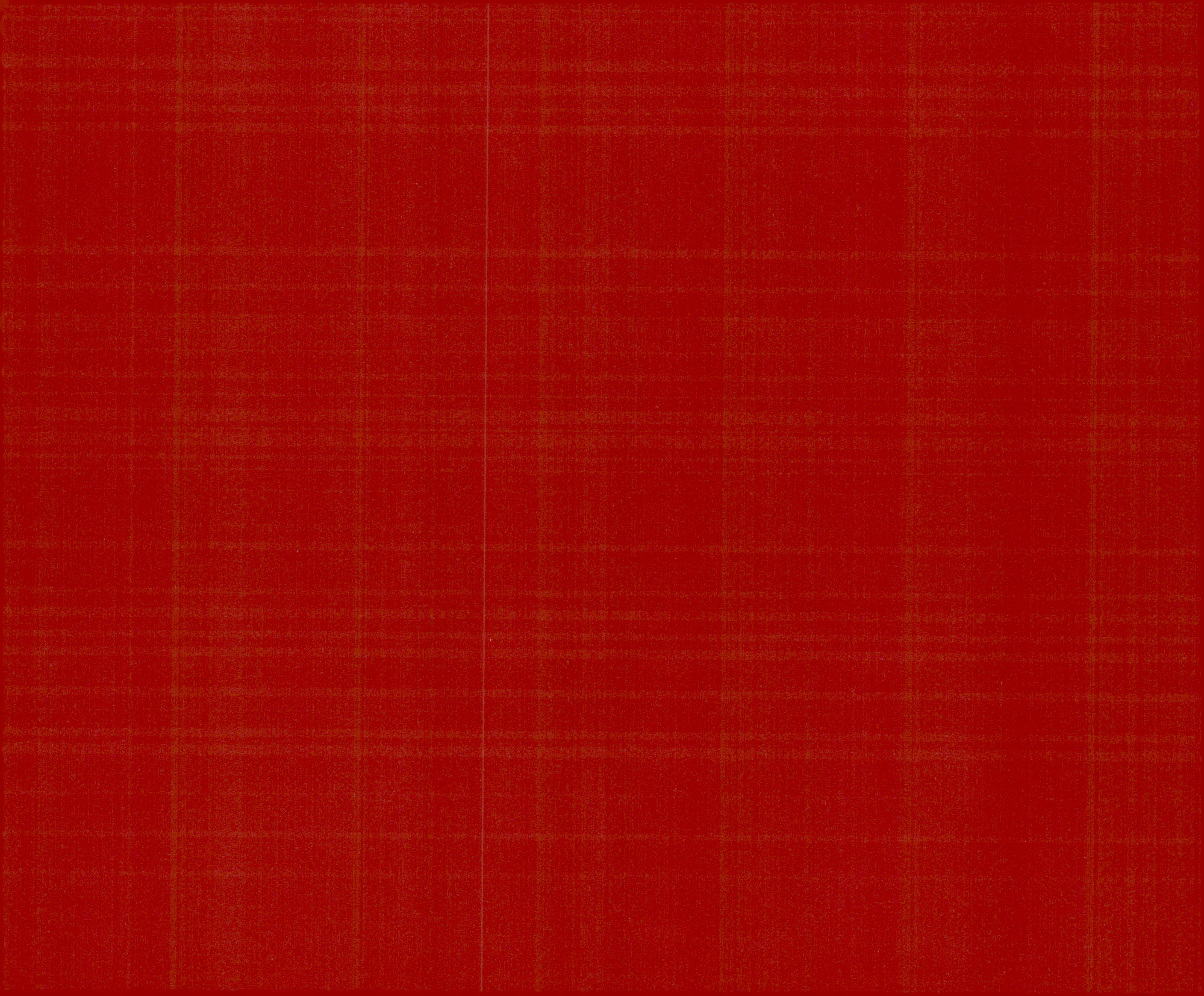

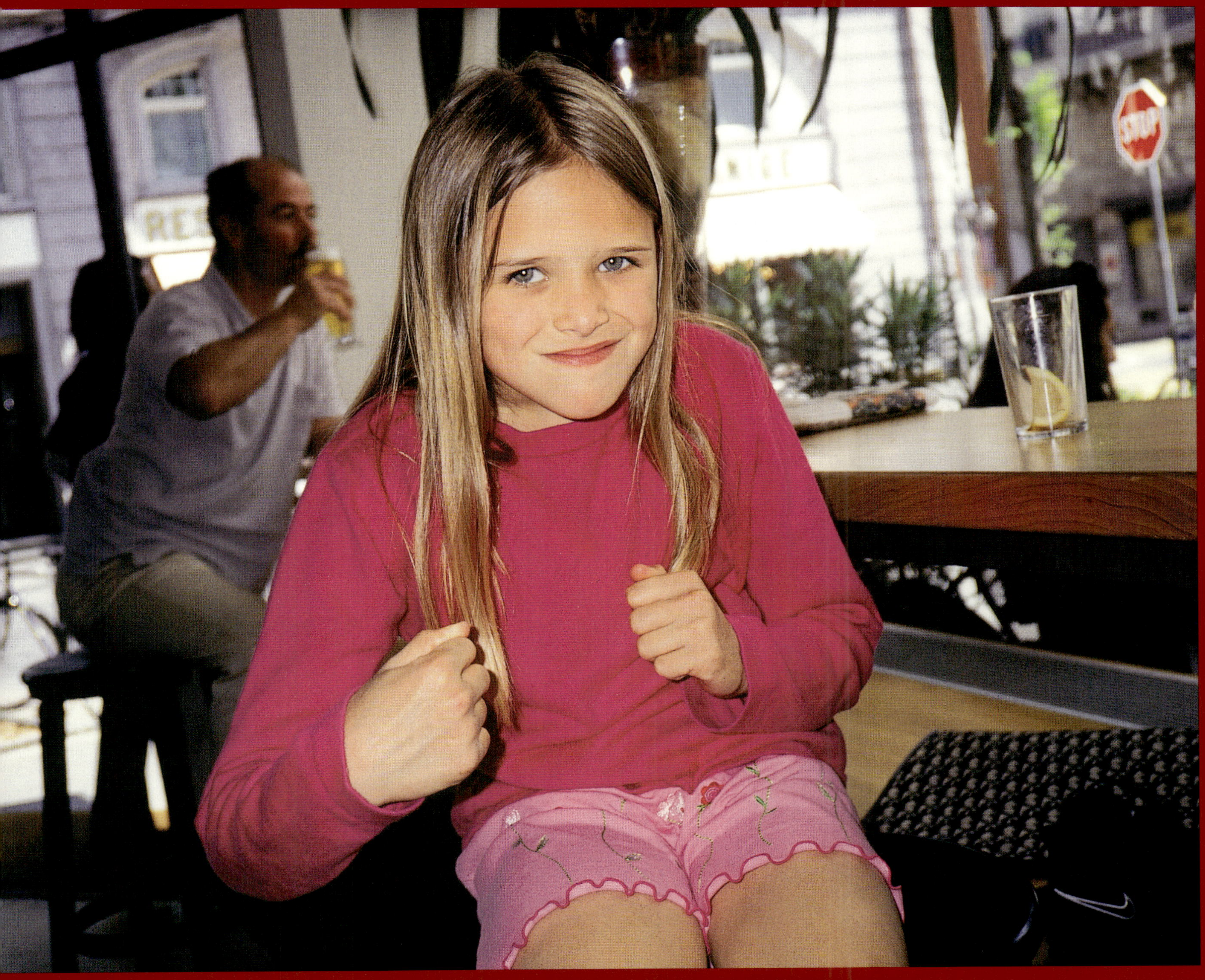

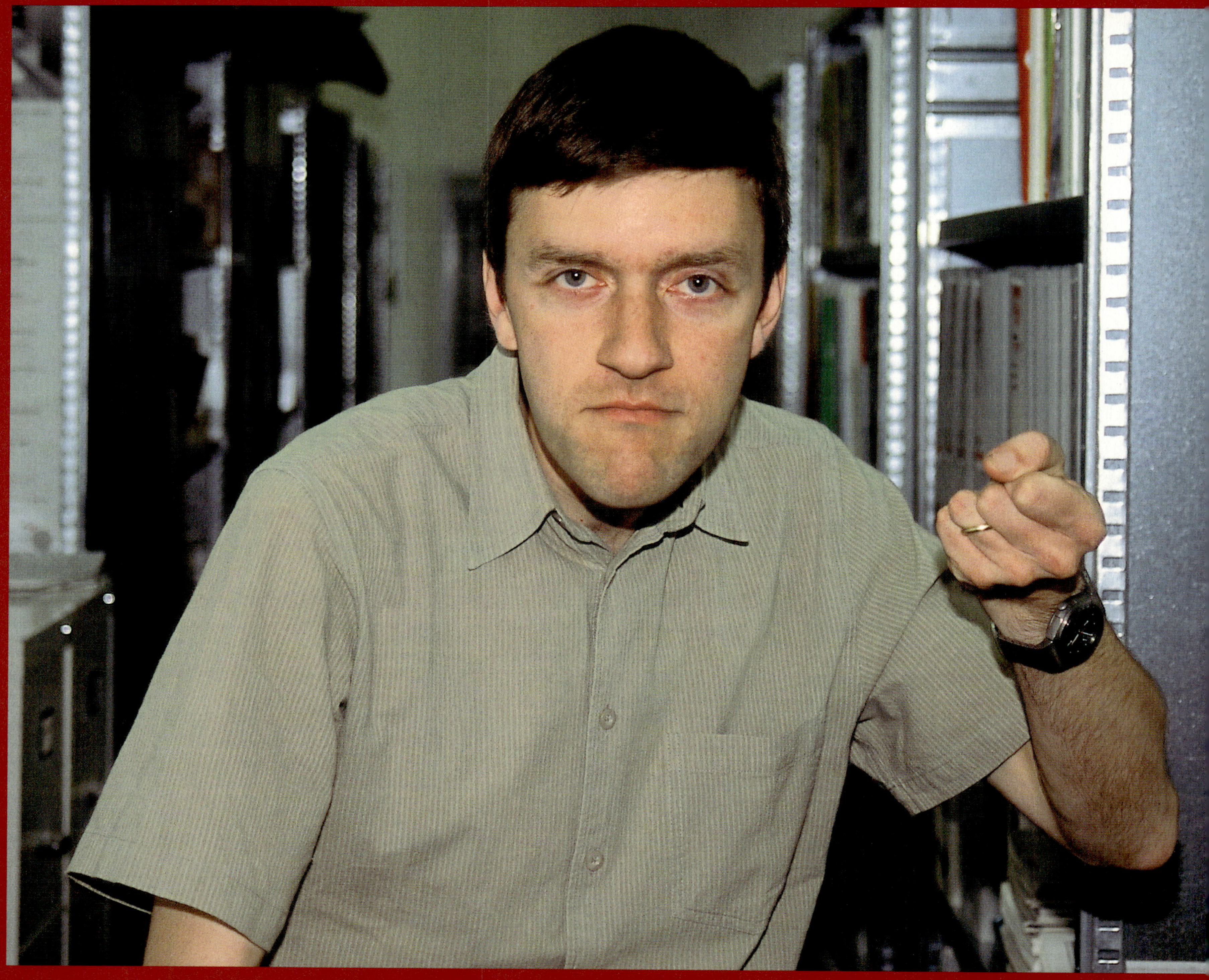

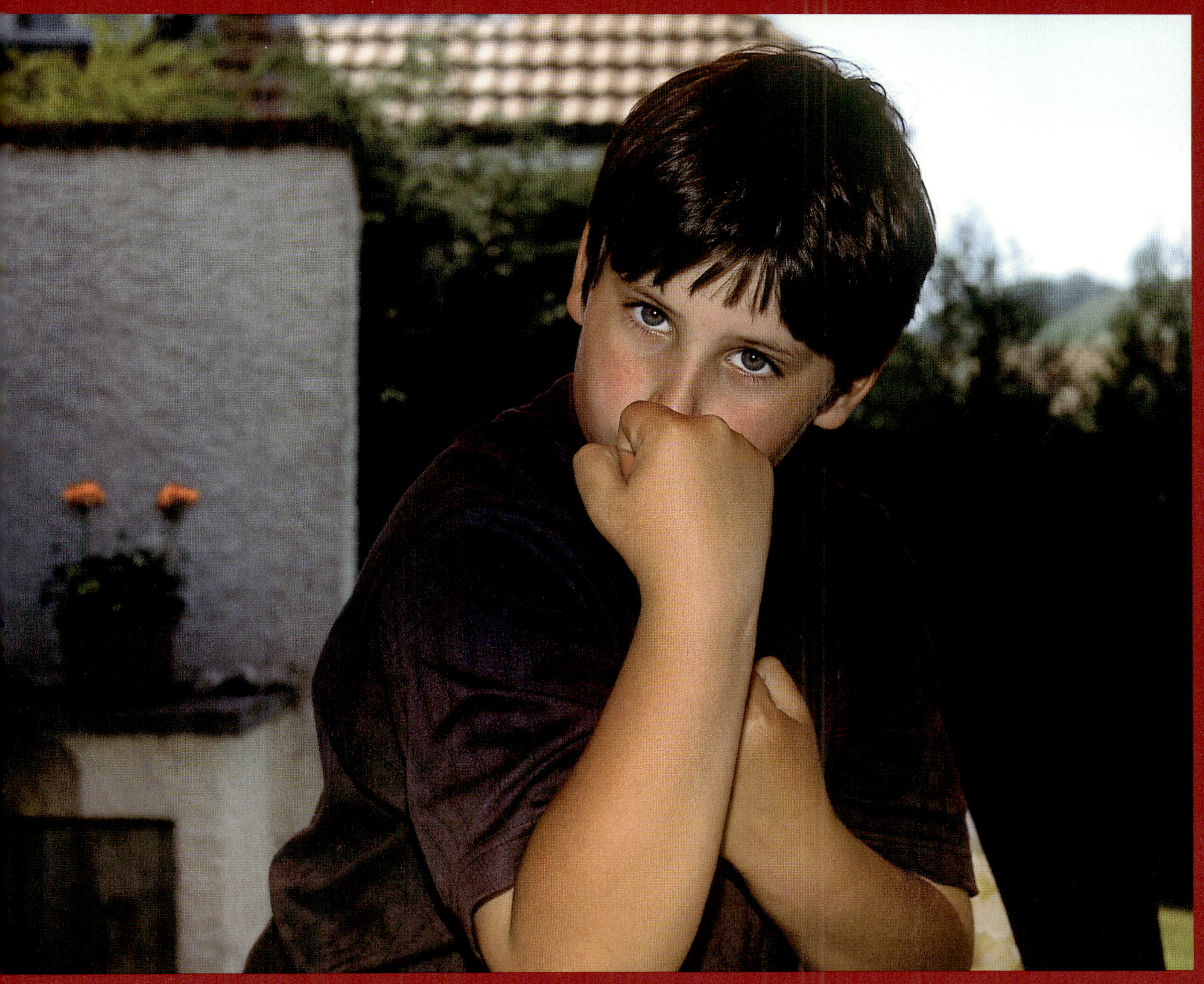

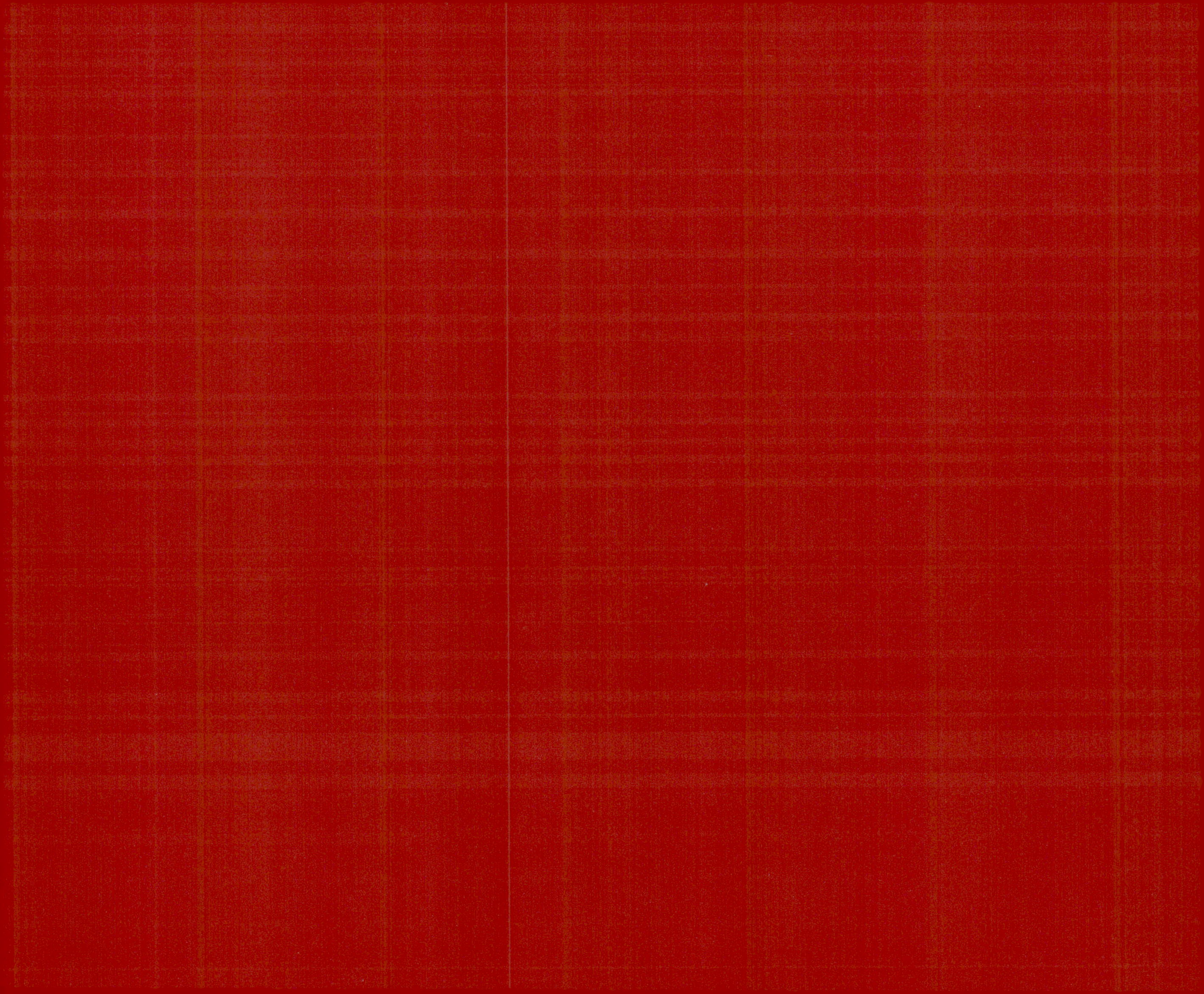

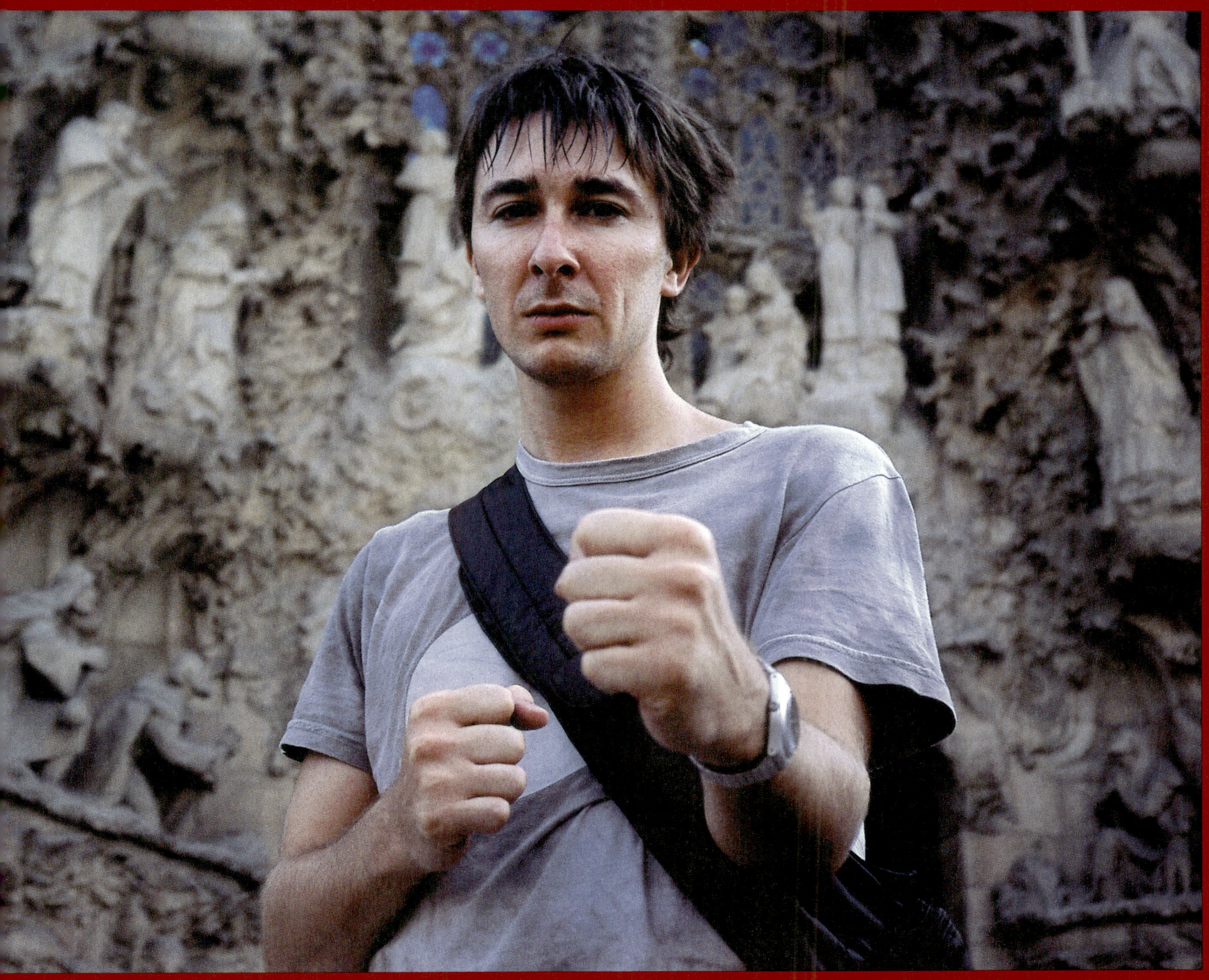

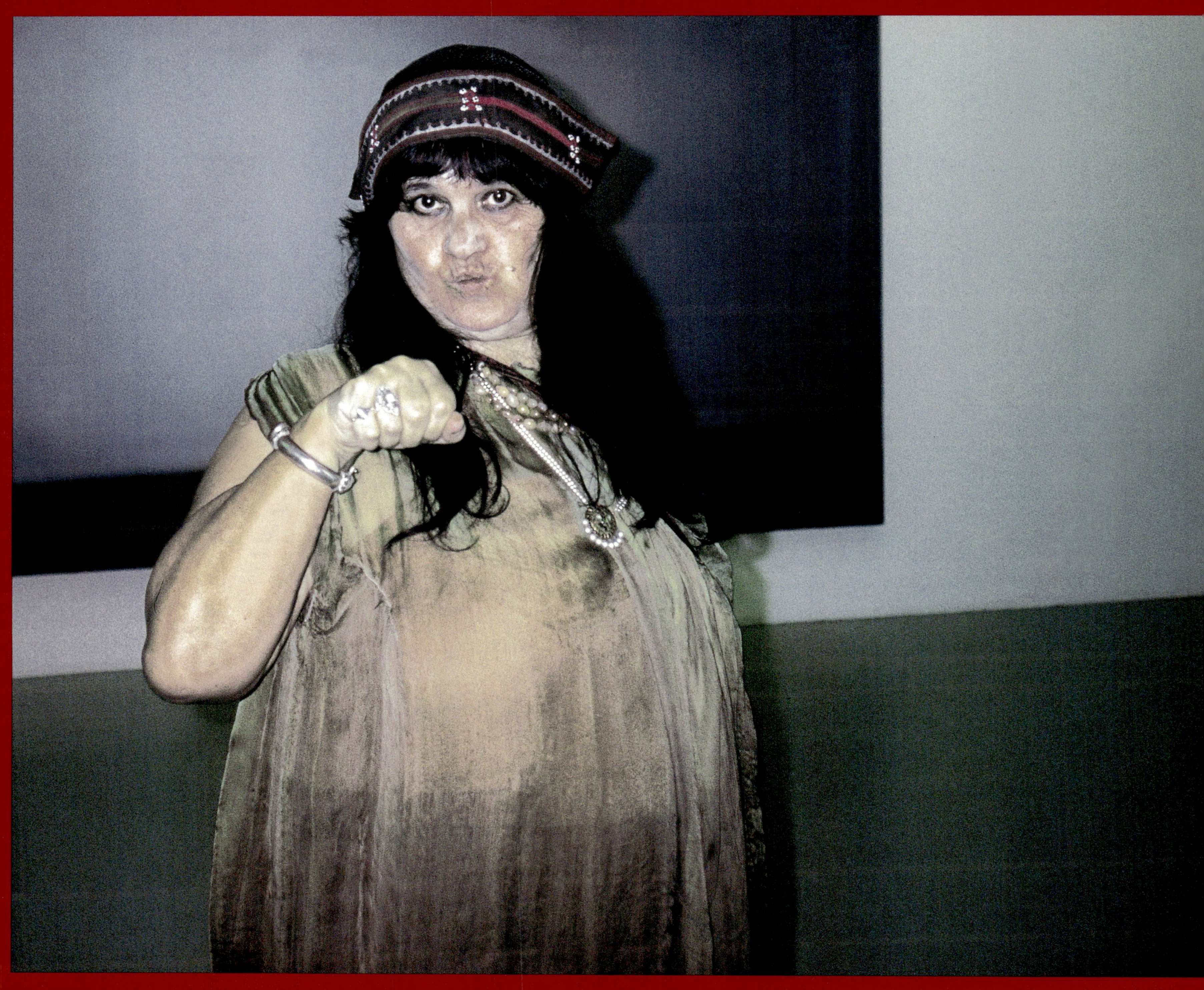

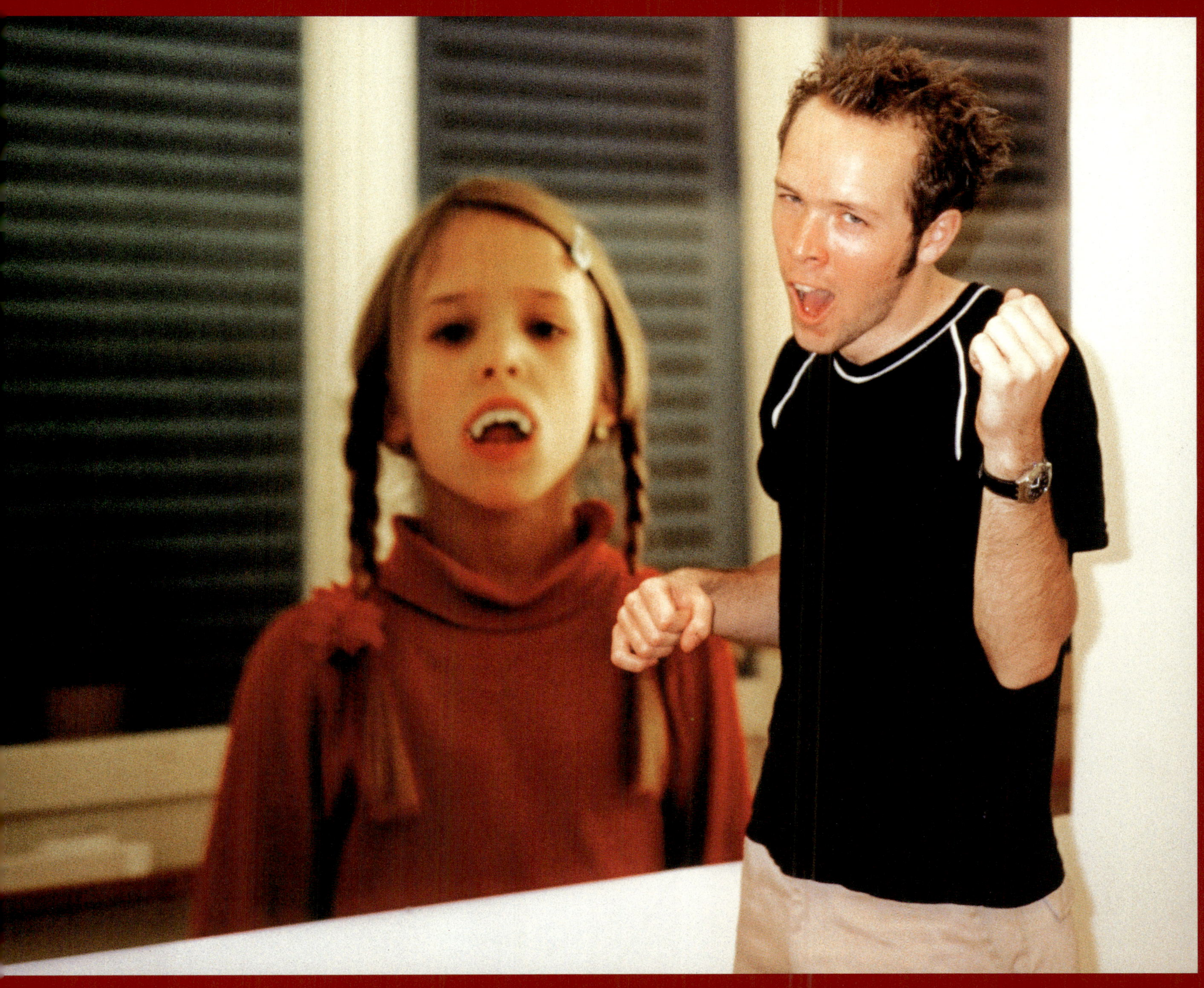

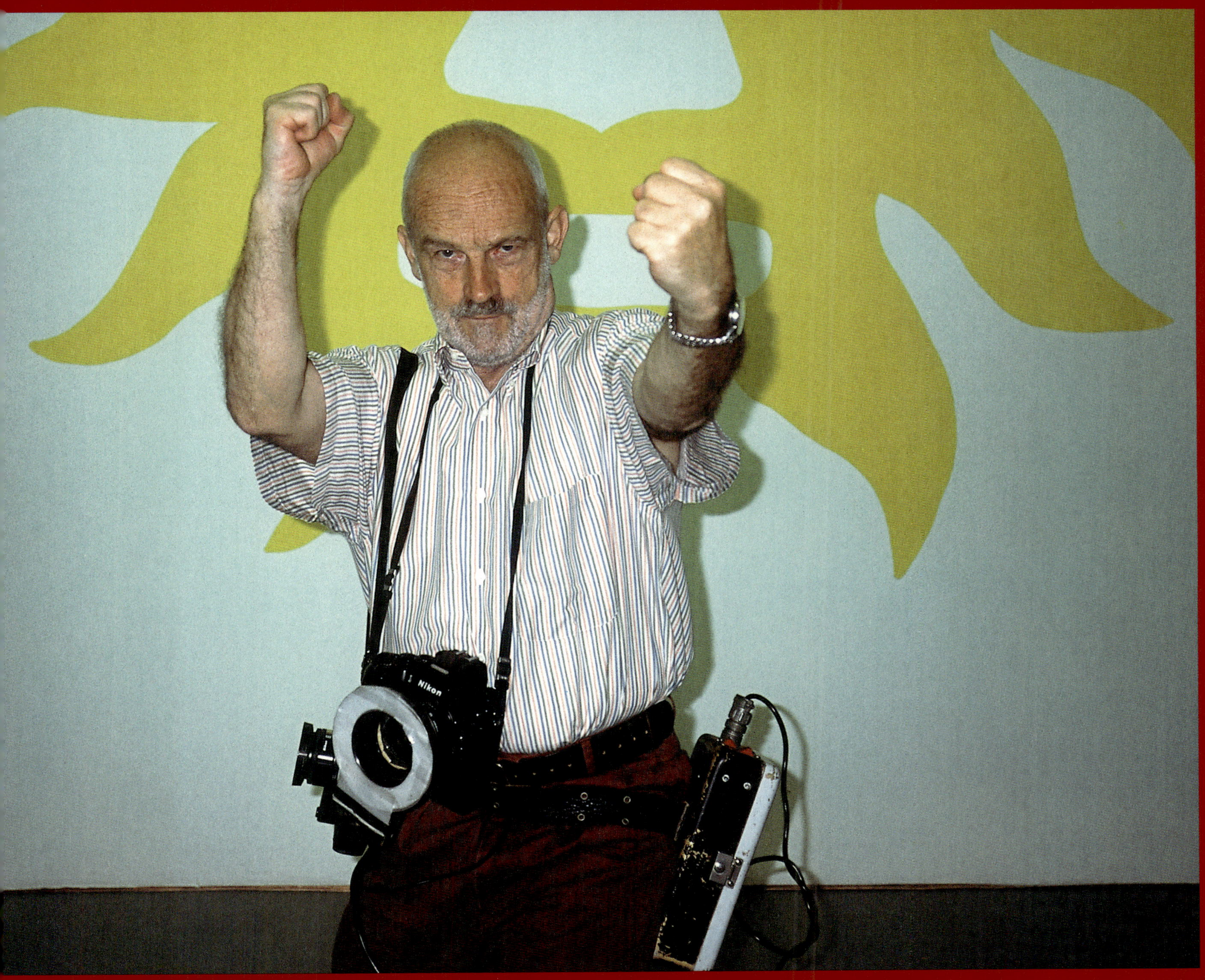
Nikon

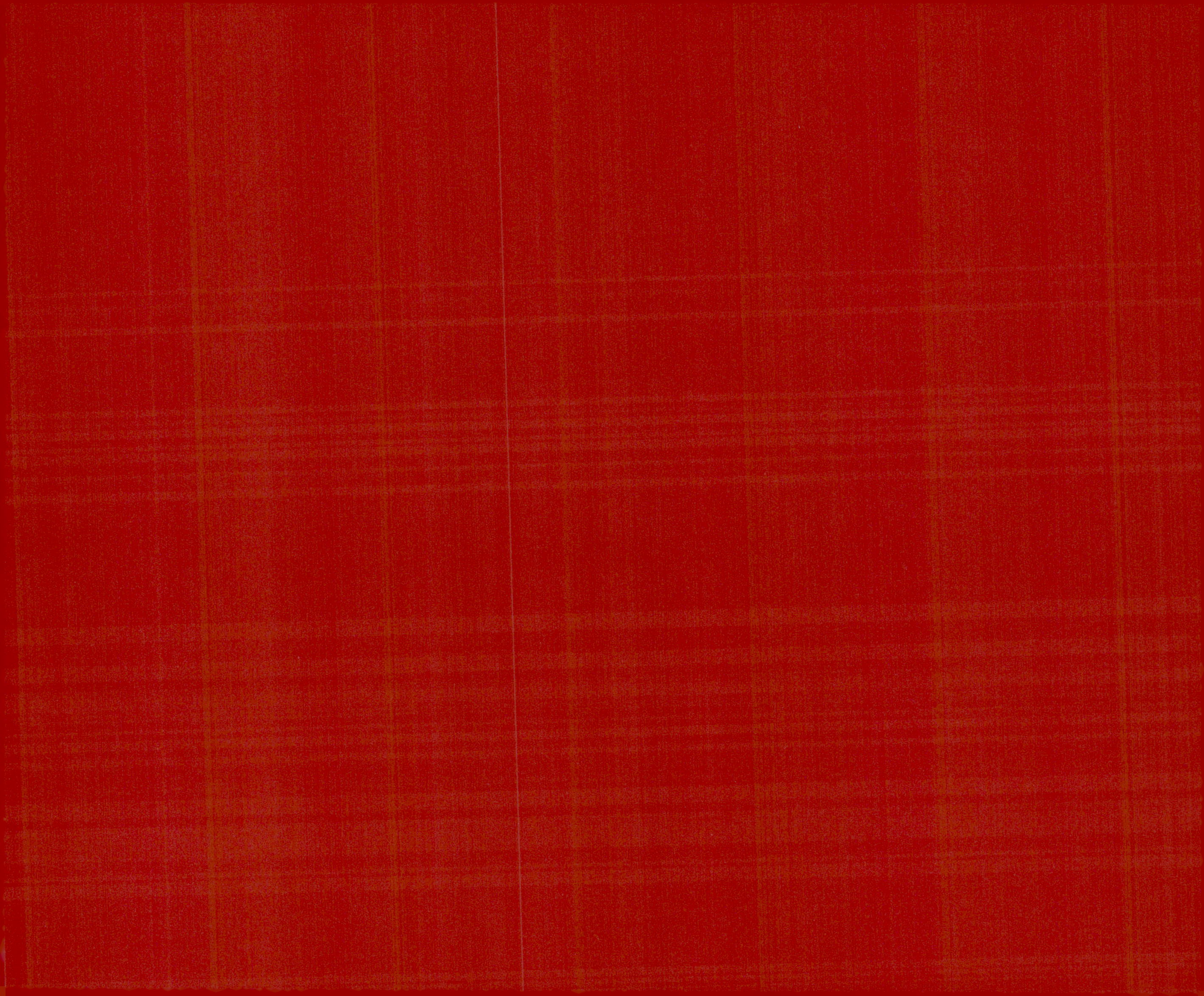

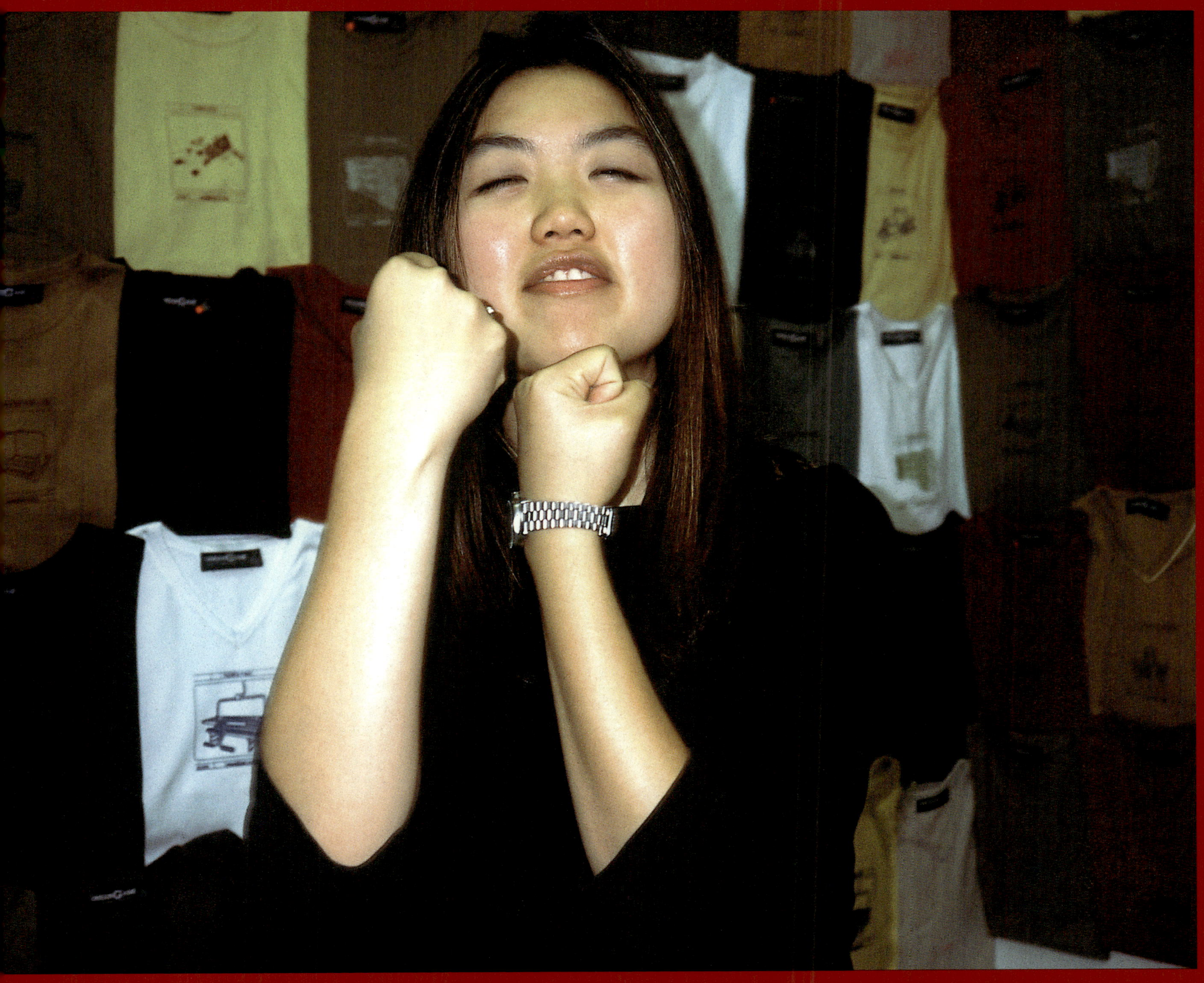

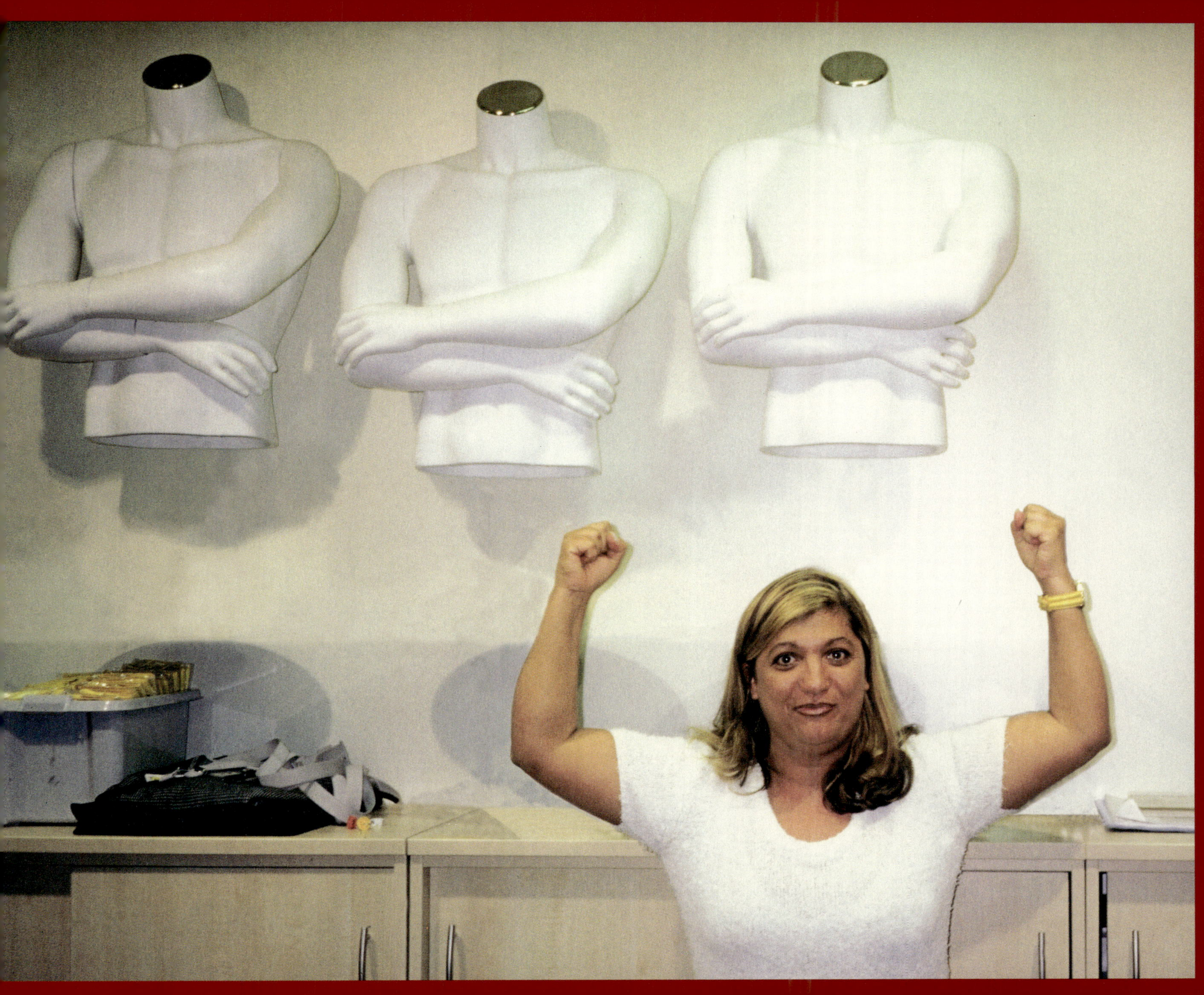

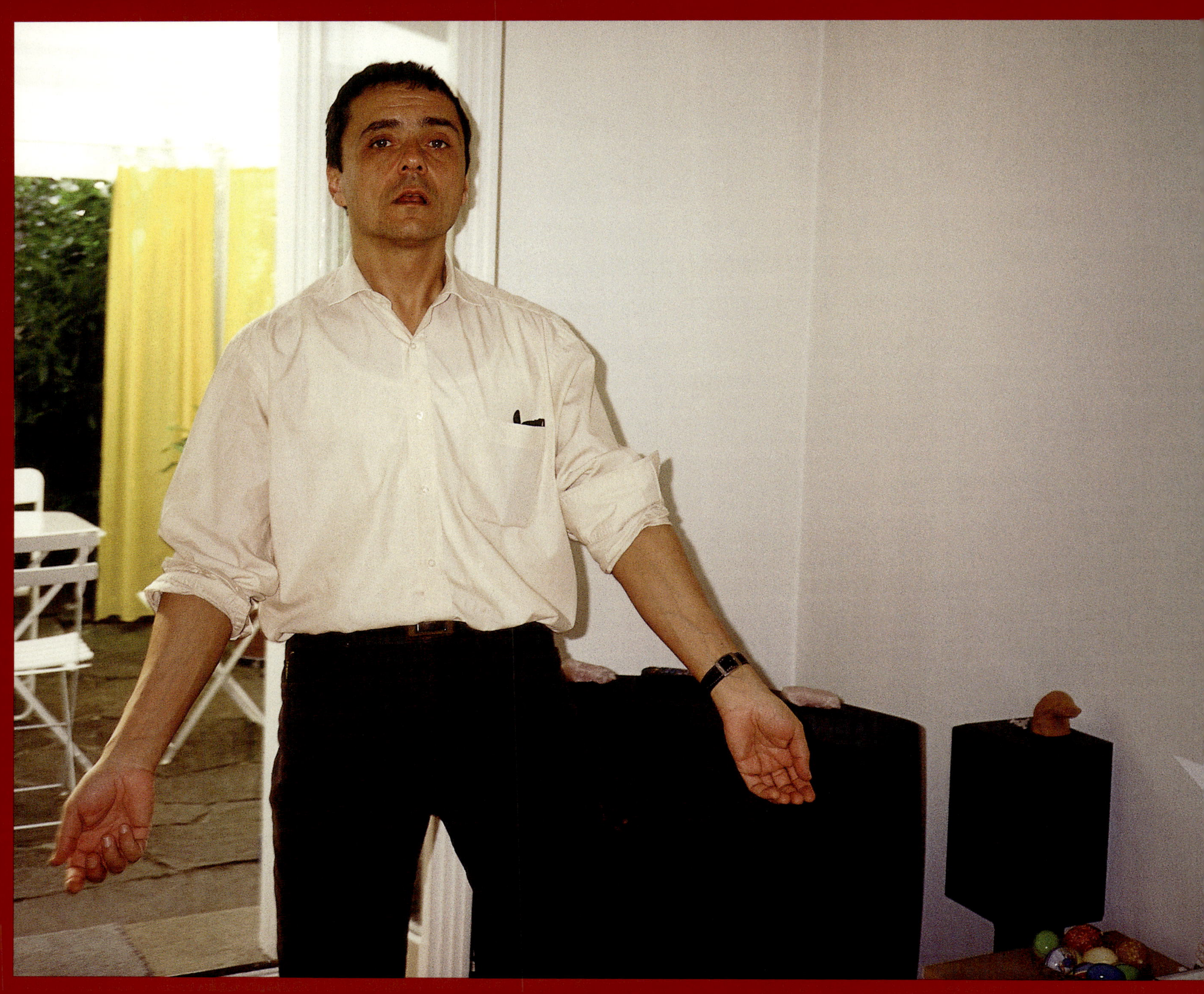

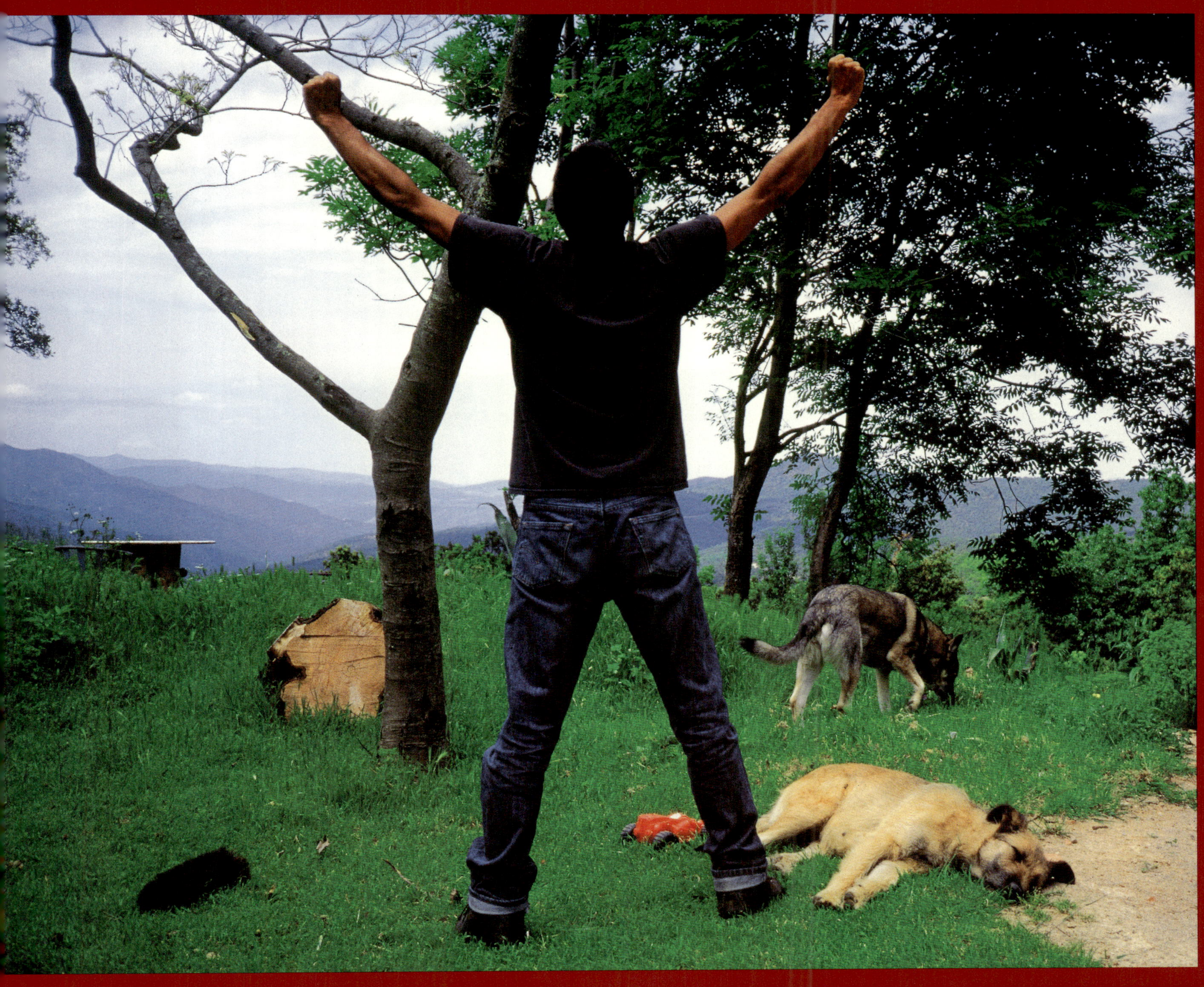

THE MUHAMMAD ALI'S

'The Muhammad Ali's' were made between 1999 and 2001 in Lucerne and Zurich and on travels to Barcelona, Perpignan, the Pyrenees, Utrecht, Venice, Paris, Berne, Geneva, Basel, St. Gall, Berlin, Innsbruck, Nuremberg and other cities. I asked more than three hundred and fifty people to give me their personal image of Muhammad Ali. Thus, I deliberately forced people into the roles of actors or imitators, so they had to react spontaneously to learn a very specific thing about themselves. This led to a different form of portrait photography. From a total of around 1000 photos, I have selected 150 for exhibition at the Kunstmuseum Luzern, the Kunsthalle Nürnberg, the Kunsthalle Tirol in Hall near Innsbruck, the Galerie Bob Gysin, Zurich, and the Galerie Kabinett, Berne. 100 of these portraits will be shown at the Espace d'Art Contemporain 'Halle au Poisson' in Perpignan in autumn 2002. This book collects sixty-three photographs and two works (pp. 1 & 88) from the 'Float like a butterfly, sting like a bee' series from 2000.

THANKS

The artist would like to thank warmly all the 'Muhammad Ali's' who spontaneously agreed to have their picture taken for this project. His thanks also go to all those people who helped, financially and spiritually, to produce this book, especially his wife Sabine Mey, his children Jonathan and Lena, Alfred Richterich Stiftung, Laufen; Zuger Kulturstiftung Landis & Gyr; Marlies & Fritz Ammann, Frauenfeld; Friedrich Christian Flick, Flick Collection, Zurich; Stadt Luzern; Kanton Luzern; Gemeinnützige Gesellschaft der Stadt Luzern; Uli Sigg, Banfa AG, Mauensee; Liechti Graf Zumsteg Architekten, Brugg; Michael Krethlow, Kabinett, Bern; Margrit & Peter Studer, Rüschlikon; and also Hanna Widrig; Franz Kurzmeyer; Walter Horcher; Ulrich Loock; Bruno Müller-Meyer; Hubert Salden; Ellen Seifermann; Andrea Madesta; Elke Schloter; Hilde Teerlinck; Erich Weiss; Erich Keiser; Anke & Thomas Wulffen; Christoph Doswald; Matthias Hafner; Marianne Grob; Patrick Frey; Simon Lenz; Urs Meile; Mirjam Varadinis and Manfred Rothenberger.

SPECIAL EDITION

Edition one: The book with the front and back cover photographs, 18 x 23 cm each, lambda print mounted behind glass, edition of 15, 2000/2002; Edition two: The book with the works on the first and on the last page from the 'Float like a butterfly, sting like a bee' series, 18 x 23 cm each, lambda print mounted behind glass, edition of 15, 2000/2002.

ABOUT THIS PUBLICATION

Editor: Mirjam Varadinis, Curator Kunsthaus Zurich. Publisher: Verlag für moderne Kunst Nürnberg. Editing: Manfred Rothenberger. Design and Photography: Stefan Banz. Reprographics: Druckerei Odermatt AG, Dallenwil, Switzerland, and DZA Satz und Bild GmbH, Altenburg, Germany. Print and Binding: Druckerei zu Altenburg GmbH, Germany. Edition: 2,000 copies. Typeface: Akzidenz Grotesk and Courier New. Paper: LuxoArtSilk, 135 gm^2, and Luxokay, 170 gm^2. © 2002 by Verlag für moderne Kunst Nürnberg & Stefan Banz. All rights reserved. Printed in Germany. ISBN 3-933096-80-4

Die Deutsche Bibliothek – CIP-Einheitsaufnahme / German Library Cataloguing-in-Publication Data
Ein Titeldatensatz für diese Publikation ist bei Der Deutschen Bibliothek erhältlich / A catalogue record for this book is available from Die Deutsche Bibliothek